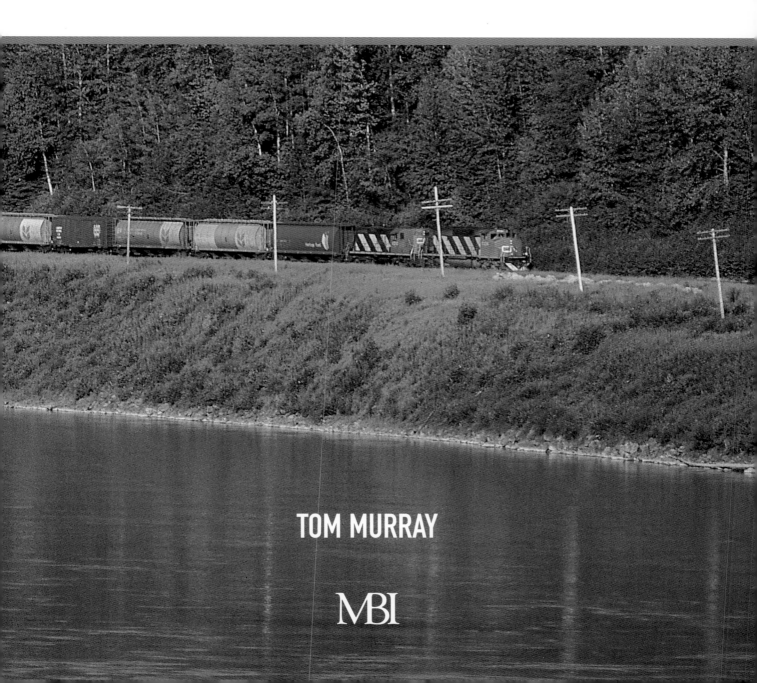

CANADIAN NATIONAL
RAILWAY

TOM MURRAY

MBI

Dedication

This book is dedicated to the memory of my father, Thomas M. Murray, who introduced me to railroads, and who influenced me in more ways than he ever knew.

This edition first published in 2004 by MBI, an imprint of MBI Publishing Company, Galtier Plaza, Suite 200, 380 Jackson Street, St. Paul, MN 55101-3885 USA

© Tom Murray, 2004

ISBN 0-7603-1764-X

Front Cover: Canadian National No. 6506 leads the *Super Continental* at Saskatoon, Saskatchewan, on January 18, 1970. *Tom Murray*

Frontis: For many years, CN used the slogan shown on the cover of this 1936 map (as well as the shorter "Serves All Canada") on boxcars and other equipment to advertise the fact that it served every one of the country's provinces. *Author collection*

Title page: In the 1970s, the Canadian government started to finance new covered hoppers to replace railroad-owned boxcars traditionally used for grain. Here, a grain train with both car types, destined for the port of Prince Rupert, passes through Prince George, British Columbia, in August 1981. *Steve Patterson*

Back cover, top: The last surviving Grand Trunk Western F3, No. 9013, was transferred to CN in 1972 for an F7 rebuilding program. It reemerged in 1973 as CN 9171, shown here as the trailing unit on a CN locomotive consist at Kitwanga, British Columbia, in October 1978. *Stan Smaill*
Bottom: Canadian National Railways timetable, April 27–October 25, 1958. *Author collection*

Edited by Dennis Pernu
Designed by Chris Fayers

Printed in Hong Kong

CONTENTS

from the United States by the time I rode one from Montreal to Jasper, Alberta; boxcab electrics hauling commuter trains into Central Station, Montreal; and white flags on extra trains. In the innovative category were the Turbo train between Montreal and Toronto, in which the passenger lucky enough to get a seat in the forward dome could look over the engineer's shoulder; the advanced "comfort cab" design that CN pioneered, which first appeared on production diesels in 1973; and a corporate logo that looks as modern today as it did when introduced in 1961.

The purpose of this book is to give an overview of CN's history, beginning with its formation in the second decade of the twentieth century, and to show how that history affected and was influenced by the regions it served. Given the company's geographic reach and the variety of freight, passenger, and non-rail operations conducted under the CN banner, a much larger volume would be required to do justice to the company, its employees and managers, and the communities it has served. Nevertheless, my hope for this book is that it will take the reader to places both familiar and not so familiar, and show how the events of years past have influenced today's CN.

A note on nomenclature: The plural "Canadian National Railways" was used on equipment and company publications for many years, and the company was commonly referred to as "CNR" by both employees and the general public. By the 1970s, the simpler "Canadian National" (*Canadien National* in French) began to appear, reflecting two corporate trends: diversification and bilingualism. Today the company is formally known as Canadian National Railway Company. It uses "CN" as its corporate identity, which is how we will refer to the company in this book.

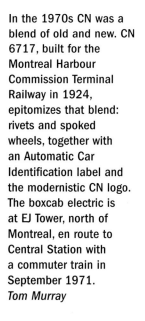

In the 1970s CN was a blend of old and new. CN 6717, built for the Montreal Harbour Commission Terminal Railway in 1924, epitomizes that blend: rivets and spoked wheels, together with an Automatic Car Identification label and the modernistic CN logo. The boxcab electric is at EJ Tower, north of Montreal, en route to Central Station with a commuter train in September 1971. *Tom Murray*

CN crews chat before departing from Brockville, Ontario, in August 1958.
The locomotive, CN 6258, is a 4-8-4 Northern built by Montreal Locomotive
Works in 1944. *Jim Shaughnessy*

Canadian Northern was 30 years behind Canadian Pacific in building through the Thompson and Fraser River canyons of British Columbia. The Thompson River flows into the Fraser at Lytton, British Columbia. Here, westbound train No. 201 crosses the Fraser at Cisco, British Columbia, 9 miles (15 kilometers) south of Lytton in May 1985. The lead locomotive is above the CP mainline. *Phil Mason*

CHAPTER ONE

THE BIRTH OF CANADIAN NATIONAL

The formation of Canadian National did not take place in a single day, or even in a single year. In fact, it consumed almost eight years, beginning in May 1915, when the Canadian Government Railways, which had been operating the Intercolonial and Prince Edward Island Railways for more than four decades, took on the additional task of running the National Transcontinental Railway.

A Grand Trunk train prepares to depart from Toronto in April 1915. *John Boyd/National Archives of Canada/ PA-061436*

In 1917 the government added one more railway, the Canadian Northern, to its portfolio, and in December 1918, the name Canadian National Railways was first authorized for use by the government railway system. The following March, Canada's minister of railways was appointed receiver of the Grand Trunk Pacific, which also became part of the government's rail network.

Three months later, in June 1919, Canadian National Railway Company was incorporated as a holding company for its various operating companies, which were known collectively as Canadian National Railways. This is often used as CN's official date of birth. However, its formative period did not end until January 1923, when the holding company acquired control of the Grand Trunk Railway.

The immediate reason that Canadian National came into existence was that the plans of early–twentieth century railroad builders and politicians had failed; their visions of prosperity and growth had been thwarted by war, recession, and their own extravagance. However, the roots of Canadian National and the reason for its existence go back much earlier. In the nineteenth century building a railway was a source of civic pride and, for many builders, a profitable enterprise. The Canadian government believed that it had a responsibility to unite the country, to foster economic development, and to promote immigration from overseas as well as westward migration by its citizens. For these reasons it generously subsidized the construction of railways.

By 1900, however, Canada already had too much trackage. In some cases, a railroad, once built, would justify its existence by generating revenues greater than its expenses. In other cases, an economic return wasn't even part of the business plan.

To understand how CN came into being, it is important to look at its predecessors, each of which made a distinct contribution to the network of rail lines that, by 1923, was being operated under the Canadian National banner.

CN's Predecessors

Intercolonial Railway

Canada's first venture into public ownership and operation of a railway began with Confederation in 1867, when Ontario, Quebec, New Brunswick, and Nova Scotia joined to form the Dominion of Canada.

One of the conditions set by the two maritime provinces was that the government would agree to build and operate a railway from a connection with Grand Trunk Railway at Rivière-du-Loup, Quebec, to Truro, Nova Scotia, where it would connect with a pre-existing rail line to Halifax. Collectively, these lines were designated the Intercolonial Railway.

After Prince Edward Island became part of Canada in 1873, the Intercolonial was

Intercolonial Railway and Prince Edward Island Railway timetable, October 1909. *Author collection*

given the job of completing the island's railway, which had been started in 1871. Both the Rivière-du-Loup–Truro mainline and the Prince Edward Island Railway were completed in 1875.

The Intercolonial, like the Grand Trunk, had originally been built to a gauge of 5 feet, 6 inches. Proponents of the wide gauge believed that it helped keep shippers loyal to one railway, but the benefits of interchangeable equipment soon won the day; following completion in 1875, the Intercolonial converted to standard gauge, 4 feet, 8½ inches. The following year, through service between Halifax and Quebec began, and in 1879 the Intercolonial purchased the Grand Trunk line from Rivière-du-Loup to Lévis, across the St. Lawrence River from Quebec City. Ten years later, the Intercolonial acquired running rights from Lévis to Montreal.

The Intercolonial was not conceived or built as a for-profit venture, and it showed, both in the route it followed and in the company's

This view depicts an arch culvert under construction on the Intercolonial Railway at Black River, Nova Scotia, in August 1871. *National Archives of Canada/PA-021995*

Intercolonial Railway locomotive 249 at Rivière-du-Loup, Quebec, in 1906. *National Archives of Canada/PA-143283*

Canadian Northern
Railway timetable,
October 1909.
*Canadian Railroad
Historical Association*

financial results. Theoretically, the route was selected on the basis of providing service to important centers of commerce; in reality, it was selected according to which local politician had the most pull. Between Moncton, New Brunswick, and Quebec City, the Intercolonial's route went farther north than it needed to, away from the border with Maine, in part because politicians in Canada and Great Britain feared that the United States might try to push the international border northward into New Brunswick. But the Intercolonial did what its founders intended it to do: It promoted the development of the region it served and helped to unify the maritime provinces with the rest of Canada.

Canadian Northern Railway

By the 1890s Canadian Pacific's (CP) monopoly in the prairie provinces was doing what monopolies often do—inspiring competitors. Combined with the government's desire to promote the settlement of the northern prairies, CP's monopoly gave William Mackenzie and Donald Mann the incentive to build the Canadian Northern Railway (CNoR).

The Mackenzie and Mann partnership started in 1895 with the construction of the Winnipeg Great Northern Railway, a 123-mile (197-kilometer) line between Gladstone and Winnipegosis, Manitoba. By 1899 the CNoR had been chartered, and it was building

at MAIR STATION   No. 9.
                                                                                   Foote

Shovels were (and are) an indispensable part of winter railroading on the prairies, as shown in this undated photo of CNoR 2036 at Mair, Saskatchewan. The Canadian Northern-style numberplate shown on this locomotive was later adopted by Canadian National. *National Archives of Canada/ C-034313*

toward Prince Albert and Saskatoon, in the area of the Northwest Territories that would become the province of Saskatchewan in 1905. The company also had in its employ David Blythe Hanna, who 20 years later would become the first president of Canadian National.

Once they had a foothold in the prairies, the next step for Mackenzie and Mann was to expand toward Lake Superior. By 1902 they had built a line southeast from Winnipeg. After crossing into Minnesota and running along the southern shore of Lake of the Woods, it entered Ontario at Rainy River and terminated at Port Arthur (which many years later would combine with the adjacent Fort William to form Thunder Bay).

Determined to break the CP's dominance in Manitoba, in the early 1900s Mackenzie and Mann leased 313 miles (504 kilometers) of track that had been built by

Northern Pacific between the U.S. border, Winnipeg, and Brandon. According to CN historian G. R. Stevens, they also built 18 branchlines totaling 614 miles (989 kilometers) in the province, making CNoR the largest railway in Manitoba.

Mackenzie and Mann continued to push west, adding trackage to their system and stimulating development on the prairies. The CNoR mainline reached Edmonton, Alberta, in 1905. By 1906, Stevens notes, 132 prairie towns and villages had been built along new Canadian Northern lines. That year CNoR bought a CP-operated line between Regina and Prince Albert, Saskatchewan, which "provided an invaluable north-south spine for branchline construction . . . . In its first year it provided its new owners with 6,000,000 bushels of grain for delivery at lakehead."

By this time Mackenzie and Mann had also turned their sights on eastern Canada. In

The former Canadian Northern line between Winnipeg, Manitoba, and Port Arthur, Ontario (today's Thunder Bay), crosses approximately 40 miles (64 kilometers) of northern Minnesota forest. A grain train passes through Roosevelt, Minnesota, en route to Thunder Bay in February 1974. *Tom Murray*

1903 they bought the Great Northern Railway of Canada, a 400-mile (644-kilometer) line in Ontario and Quebec that included a branchline into Montreal from the north. Although it took them several years to acquire the necessary land, they also built a 3.2-mile (5.2-kilometer) tunnel through Mount Royal to the center of the city, which opened in 1918. In 1906 Mackenzie and Mann opened the first segment of the Canadian Northern Ontario Railway, which eventually extended from Toronto to Capreol, with various branches, including one to Sudbury.

Mackenzie and Mann's first venture in the Maritimes (aside from working on the

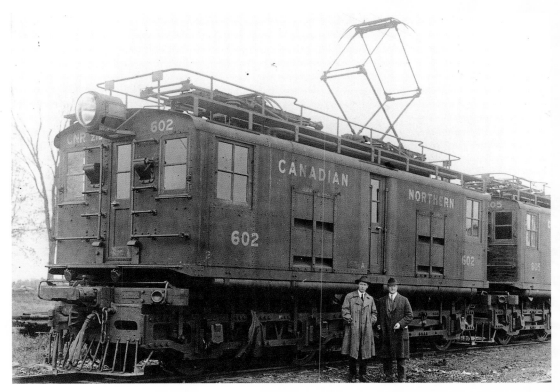

One of Canadian Northern's goals was to reach downtown Montreal, and in 1913 it began construction on a 3.2-mile (5.2-kilometer) tunnel under Mt. Royal. CNoR 602 (photographed in 1914, four years before the completion of the project) was one of six electric locomotives acquired from Canadian General Electric for this service. *National Archives of Canada/PA-164733*

Canadian Northern got its start as a farmers' railway on the prairies of Manitoba, but by 1916, when this photo of a CNoR club car was taken, it was a transcontinental enterprise. *National Archives of Canada/ C-034305*

construction of Canadian Pacific's line across Maine to Saint John, New Brunswick) was a 60-mile (97-kilometer) coal line on Cape Breton, Nova Scotia, in 1901. CNoR subsequently acquired a 99-mile (159-kilometer) package of short lines (built and unbuilt), and by 1907 it had constructed 246 additional miles (396 kilometers) of connecting trackage, all in Nova Scotia. The CNoR's main subsidiary in Nova Scotia was the Halifax & South Western Railway, which ran from Halifax to Yarmouth.

Mackenzie and Mann became determined to stitch together their eastern and western lines into a transcontinental system, and in 1911 they started construction from Montreal to Port Arthur, a distance of 1,050 miles (1,690 kilometers). Soon after, they began working their way west from Edmonton to Vancouver. The route west of Edmonton to Jasper, Alberta, and Yellowhead Pass duplicated the Grand Trunk Pacific line to Prince Rupert, British Columbia, and for many miles the two routes ran side by side.

Mackenzie and Mann, unlike some of their contemporary rail builders, had generally used economical construction standards, a practice they abandoned on the 250 miles

(402 kilometers) from Kamloops, British Columbia, to tidewater, where Stevens writes they "elected to build to an even higher specification than CP." When the Pacific route was completed in 1915, CNoR was truly a transcontinental railroad.

Mackenzie and Mann, shrewd businessmen though they were, soon found themselves overextended financially. The earning power of their new lines could not support the debt they had taken on. The outbreak of war in Europe dried up the available capital, and in 1917 CNoR was taken over by its largest creditor, the Canadian government.

Grand Trunk Railway

Although the Grand Trunk Railway (GTR) was the last company to become part of CN during the formative years of 1915 to 1923, it was the linchpin of the system, providing both the geographic reach and the density of traffic necessary to make the system economically viable.

GTR came into existence as a company in 1852 through the sponsorship of railway promoter Francis Hincks. Eventually, however,

Grand Trunk Railway/Grand Trunk Pacific timetable, July 1912. *Author collection*

The morning train from Sherbrooke, Quebec, to Montreal roars through Bromptonville, Quebec, behind CN 4-6-2 No. 5288 in February 1957. The temperature is -24 degrees Fahrenheit (-31 degrees Celsius). Bromptonville is on the former GTR line between Montreal and Portland, Maine. *Jim Shaughnessy*

it acquired railways with even earlier beginnings, including Canada's first railway, a 14-mile (23-kilometer) line between St. John and La Prairie, Quebec, 8 miles (13 kilometers) upstream from Montreal, that opened in 1836. The line was later extended 20 additional miles (32 kilometers) to Rouses Point, New York.

Hincks' vision involved connecting Canada with the United States, or more specifically, connecting U.S. cities through Canada. He planned a railroad that would extend from Portland, Maine, to Chicago, via Quebec and Ontario. When completed, the Portland–Chicago route would be 1,150 miles (1,851 kilometers) in length, 659 miles (1,061 kilometers) of it in Canada. Hincks' plan was beneficial to some constituencies in each country. Portland benefited because the Canadian route was shorter than any all-U.S. rail route to the west. Montreal liked the plan, because Portland was the nearest all-weather port. The losers were Nova Scotia and New Brunswick, both of which had all-weather ports of their own.

Clearing the Grand Trunk line at Chaudière, Quebec, 9 miles (15 kilometers) southwest of Lévis, in February 1869.
Alexander Henderson/ National Archives of Canada/PA-149764

Hincks proved to be a better promoter than businessman, and GTR ran into financial trouble early on. When the dust settled, company control was in the hands of British financiers, and would remain there until CN took control of the company after World War I. For the balance of the nineteenth century, however, the company's management was to be based in London, England.

Despite financial challenges, GTR opened for business in 1856 on a route from Montreal to Sarnia, Ontario, via Toronto, Hamilton, and London. In December 1859 the Victoria Bridge, 1.7 miles (2.8 kilometers) in length, spanning the St. Lawrence River at Montreal, was placed into service, completing the all-rail route to eastern Quebec and Maine.

The company did not reach Chicago until 1879, when its president, Sir Henry Tyler, outmaneuvered William Vanderbilt by purchasing several small railroads in Michigan and Indiana. In combination with trackage purchased earlier in Chicago itself, these gave GTR the western terminus it had long coveted. G. R. Stevens notes that this extension transformed the company's traffic base and finances: "Within four months of entry into Chicago, almost half the Grand Trunk's traffic originated in that city." Initially, rail traffic was ferried between Sarnia and Port Huron, Michigan, but in 1891 the St. Clair Tunnel opened to create an all-rail route to Chicago.

In the meantime GTR's role as a bridge route between U.S. connections was cemented

Grand Trunk completed the double-tracking of its line between Montreal and Toronto in 1892, and it remains one of the busiest rail segments in Canada. This train is passing through Kingston, Ontario, in August 1991. *Phil Mason*

Railway grading as it was practiced circa 1910. This scene is on the route of the National Transcontinental, east of Nipigon Lake, Ontario. *National Archives of Canada/C-025623*

in 1882 with the acquisition of the Great Western Railway, whose mainline ran from Niagara Falls to Windsor, a route it had opened in 1854. The Great Western's line to Sarnia was better than GTR's own line, and would eventually become a key segment in GTR's (and CN's) mainline. GTR became the seventh-largest North American railroad, measured by mileage.

Fueled by the profits from its Chicago traffic, GTR continued to expand. In 1883, it raised its profile in New England by buying a 50 percent interest in the Central Vermont, which helped it win traffic to Boston (via the Boston & Maine) and to New York City (via steamer from New London, Connecticut). GTR acquired full control of Central Vermont in 1898.

GTR also extended its presence north and northwest of Toronto toward Lake Huron and Lake Nipissing, and it completed the double-tracking of its Montreal–Toronto mainline in 1892. By 1893 GTR lines extended throughout southwestern Ontario; north to North Bay; west across Michigan to Grand Rapids, Grand Haven, and Muskegon (including a ferry service to Milwaukee), as well as Chicago; and east to Rivière-du-Loup, Quebec, and Portland Maine.

As well positioned as it was, GTR's power to control its own destiny was constrained by geographic limitations and competitive realities. Canadian Pacific completed its transcontinental mainline in 1885. By then CP was already looking to the industrial heartland of Canada—southern Ontario—for expansion opportunities. Its first acquisition (but not its last) in GTR's backyard was the Credit Valley Railway between Toronto and Woodstock. CP would not make it easy for GTR to move traffic to and from the west—CP wanted 100 percent of the haul.

Grand Trunk had been offered the opportunity to build the transcontinental railway, but had turned it down. As the nineteenth century turned into the twentieth, GTR's management began to reconsider that decision. It wanted to be in the West.

Grand Trunk Pacific Railway and National Transcontinental Railway

The Grand Trunk Pacific (GTP) and the National Transcontinental were separate railways, legally and financially, but they were conceived as a single continuous line of railroad from Moncton, New Brunswick, to Prince Rupert, British Columbia, and their histories are interwoven.

The life span of the two railways consumed only a little more than a decade from start to finish. Their roots are in a 1903 proposal by GTR's president, Charles Melville Hays, for a second transcontinental railway, running from North Bay, Ontario, to a port along the northern coast of British Columbia (ultimately, Prince Rupert). Although the Dominion government favored the proposal in general, GTR's U.S. orientation gave the government pause. It feared that if the railway were built as proposed, Canadian grain would move via Grand Trunk to Portland, Maine, for export, rather than via Canadian ports.

The government's counterproposal, which GTR accepted to its ultimate regret, was to split the project into two pieces. The

company's plan would be followed west of Winnipeg, where, with government financial aid, it would build and operate a 1,743-mile (2,805-kilometer) railway to be known as Grand Trunk Pacific.

East of Winnipeg, a new 2,019-mile (3,251-kilometer) line, the National Transcontinental, was to be built to a connection with the Intercolonial at Moncton. This line would be financed by the federal government and upon completion leased to the Grand Trunk Pacific.

The GTP line to Prince Rupert via Yellowhead Pass, located in the Rocky Mountains between Alberta and British Columbia, was completed on April 9, 1914.

In addition to its mainline and several branches west of Winnipeg, GTP built one line in the East that connected the National Transcontinental mainline at Sioux Lookout, Ontario, with Fort William, giving GTP a route to move grain from the prairies to Lake Superior.

The National Transcontinental traversed northern Ontario and Quebec through areas that were devoid of population and therefore lacking any means of access, other than the railroad itself. Yet the railway's builders insisted on the highest standards. Steel bridges were built, for example, where wooden ones would have been adequate. In combination

Grand Trunk Pacific was a latecomer to the Canadian prairies, but its mainline became part of the CN transcontinental route. This scene is at St. Lazare, Manitoba, 204.5 miles (329.1 kilometers) west of Winnipeg. GTP 67 was a 1908 product of Montreal Locomotive Works. *National Archives of Canada/ C-010723*

G.T.P. Rolling Stock
Prince Rupert B.C.

Grand Trunk Pacific built through British Columbia from both east and west. Crews on the western end began at Prince Rupert, where these locomotives are being offloaded from barges in 1910. *National Archives of Canada/PA-123743*

A Grand Trunk Pacific train departs Prince Rupert, destined to Winnipeg, in 1915. GTP locomotive No. 614 remained in service for CN until 1954, after being renumbered CN 1437. *Horatio Nelson Tapley/National Archives of Canada/PA-011231*

with inflation in the cost of both labor and materials, this led to an ultimate construction cost of $169 million, more than double the estimated cost—all for a railroad whose traffic outlook was dim at best.

When the National Transcontinental was completed in 1915, GTR refused to follow through on its agreement to lease the property, and the government took over the Winnipeg–Moncton line. It later took over GTP's line between Sioux Lookout and Fort William as well, which gave the government railway a continuous route between Lake Superior and Winnipeg.

Even without having to take financial responsibility for the National Transcontinental, by 1915 GTR was caught between the high interest charges from the debt it took on to build the GTP, and the fact that refinancing was impossible because of the war in Europe. GTR attempted to convince the government to take over the GTP, but was turned down. It was the beginning of the end for Grand Trunk.

Above left: The National Transcontinental line between Quebec City and Moncton, New Brunswick, had several high steel bridges, including this one at Cap Rouge, Quebec, photographed in 1916. *National Archives of Canada/PA-110907.* **Above:** A track-layer at work 117 miles (188 kilometers) east of Winnipeg on the National Transcontinental Railway, circa 1906. CN historian G. R. Stevens, discussing the challenges that faced the builders of the NTR, refers to "the great stony extrusions that barricaded the passage between Lake Superior and Hudson Bay." This segment of the NTR is now part of the CN mainline between Winnipeg and eastern Canada. *National Archives of Canada/C-046485*

Nationalization and Consolidation

CN historian Donald MacKay has said that in Canada "governments and railways had been so entangled, and so much tax money had been spent, that nationalization was logical if not inevitable." There were certainly missed opportunities and decisions of colossal shortsightedness that, had they gone the other way, might have postponed or even prevented nationalization.

Suppose, for example, that Mackenzie and Mann had been willing to sell the

In April 2000 CN train No. 308 crosses the Salmon River Bridge in New Denmark, New Brunswick. This is the second-longest railway bridge in Canada, and one of four large trestles the former National Transcontinental route crosses in a 30-mile (48-kilometer) stretch of track east of Grand Falls. *George Pitarys*

Canadian Northern to Grand Trunk. This would have given GTR the western access it wanted while avoiding the building of duplicate trackage in the West. The National Transcontinental was poorly conceived, and its decision to build parallel to the Intercolonial between Quebec and Moncton also represented a costly redundancy. Further, the excesses of optimism that led to the building of these railways collided with the realities of World War I, which diverted resources and capital away from domestic industries and toward the war effort.

As MacKay suggests, the undoing of the privately owned Canadian Northern and Grand Trunk systems was based largely on their dependence on public funds for construction of the western rail lines. When they got into financial trouble, the government

was able to dictate the terms of takeover. In 1917, CNoR became the first private company to become part of the expanding government rail system. The government took over responsibility for the company's debt and, after some negotiation, made a modest settlement with the company's shareholders.

The acquisition of GTR took much longer. Most of its shareholders were British, and after years of hearings, reports, and legal wrangling, they got nothing, prompting a long-lasting mistrust in the United Kingdom of the Canadian government and financial system.

With the absorption of CNoR, the government rail system had more than 14,000 miles (22,500 kilometers) of trackage. Two-thirds of the total was from CNoR, and that company's president, D. B. Hanna, was

Canadian Government Railways timetable, December 1, 1917. *Canadian Railroad Historical Association*

appointed to the same position in the new organization. Hanna was determined that CN would operate free of political interference, and for a time he succeeded. However, in 1922 William Lyon Mackenzie King became prime minister. Hanna had been appointed president by the Conservative party, and King was a Liberal. Hanna submitted his resignation. To replace him, King selected Sir Henry Thornton, an American by birth who had been running the Great Eastern Railway in England, and who had been knighted for his service during the war.

By the time Thornton became president of CN in December 1922, the company had been treating GTR as part of the system for more than two years, a relationship that became official in January 1923. The company now had more than 22,000 route miles (35,000 kilometers) and almost 100,000 employees, making it the largest railway in the world. Financially, however, CN was barely covering its operating expenses. Thornton had a big job ahead of him.

Canadian National Railways timetable, July 20, 1920. *Canadian Railroad Historical Association*

Following the retirement of CN 6218, Mountain type 6060, which had been on display at Jasper, Alberta, was restored to service in 1972. Here it crosses the Richelieu River on an excursion in September 1973. *Jim Shaughnessy*

CHAPTER TWO

THE FIRST QUARTER CENTURY: *Surviving Depression and War*

By the time Sir Henry Thornton took the helm of Canadian National Railways, the new company was showing signs of a turnaround from the financial distress that followed World War I. That distress was triggered by two factors: postwar inflation in expenses and a drop-off in business. CN's operating ratio (expenses as a percentage of revenues) peaked at 114.5 percent in 1920. Efficient, well-run railways tend to have operating ratios of about 75 percent,

The two most recognizable groups of steam locomotives on the CN roster were the five streamlined 6400 series Northerns delivered in 1936 and the 20 Mountains numbered 6060 through 6079 and delivered in 1944. The latter were CN's last new steam locomotives. CN 6079 and 6404 pose at Toronto. *Jim Shaughnessy*

and preferably lower. By 1922 CN's operating ratio was down to 98.7 percent, but this was still far too high.

One key to making CN more efficient was to integrate the lines of its predecessor companies. A notable example was the 30.7-mile (49.4-kilometer) Long Lake cutoff between the former Canadian Northern line at Longlac, Ontario, and the National Transcontinental route at Nakina, opened in September 1924. This permitted trains between Montreal and Toronto in the east and Winnipeg in the west to be operated on a more direct route, bypassing Port Arthur and the CNoR line through northern Minnesota.

CN advertisements trumpeted the company's size and geographic scope. A 1928 ad asked, "Do you know . . . the largest railway system in America is *NOT* in the United States? It is in Canada—the 22,681 miles of Canadian National Railways which span Canada from coast to coast."

CN was deriving roughly 75 percent of its revenue from freight service, but the company offered a diverse array of transportation services. A 1925 tourist brochure listed its non-rail operations: five steamers along the coast of British Columbia, four lake steamers, 11 car ferries, 102,000 miles (164,000 kilometers) of telegraph lines, 10 hotels, and an

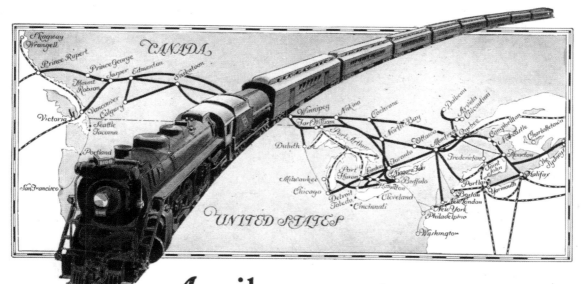

A railway system that spans a continent and links two great nations

NEW YORK and Montreal; Chicago and Toronto; Duluth and Winnipeg lie south and north of the International Line. But they are not foreign ground to the citizens of either the United States or Canada. Language, race and customs and the luxurious trains of Canadian National Railways link them together and make them neighbors.

Wherever you wish to go in Canada—whether to the playgrounds of the Maritime Provinces, Historic Quebec, the lake and forest regions of Ontario, the great prairie provinces, the mighty Canadian Rockies, to the Pacific Coast and Alaska—Canadian National will take you, speedily, comfortably and over a route replete with magnificent scenery.

But Canadian National is more than a railroad. It operates year 'round hotels and summer resorts. It provides freight, express and telegraph service with connections to all parts of the world. Canadian National Steamships carry Canada's ensign over the seven seas. Eleven Canadian National radio stations broadcast from coast to coast.

For information on Canada's natural resources and business opportunities, for tickets and accommodations, call at, write or telephone the nearest Canadian National office.

In Ottawa, Ont., the capital of the Dominion, is the Chateau Laurier, one of the distinctive hotels owned and operated by Canadian National Railways.

CANADIAN NATIONAL
The Largest Railway System in America

OPERATING RAILWAYS · STEAMSHIPS . HOTELS · TELEGRAPH AND EXPRESS SERVICE · RADIO STATIONS

Much of CN's early advertising was devoted to promoting awareness in the United States of the company's size and scope. This 1929 ad appeared in *National Geographic. Author collection*

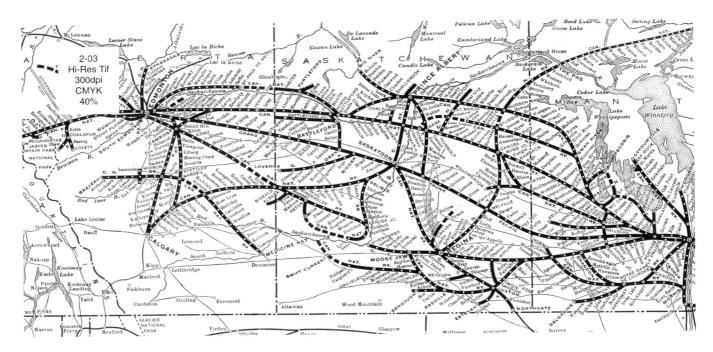

This detail of the prairie provinces is from a CN-GTR-GTP map dated March 24, 1921, during CN's formative period. It shows the heritage of CN's prairie branchlines: Those marked "Can. Nat. Ry." are former Canadian Northern routes, while GTP lines are labeled as such. *Author collection*

Opposite: CN 3496 at Fort Erie, Ontario, in August 1957. This engine was built in 1913 for Grand Trunk Railway and was retired in 1960, the same year that CN ceased regular steam operations. *Jim Shaughnessy*

express company. CN also managed Canada's merchant marine, consisting of 57 vessels operating in worldwide service.

Although rail passenger service generated only 15 percent of CN's revenues, CN did its best to improve the returns from this business. In 1923 a radio service was started to provide entertainment and news for passengers on CN trains. This gave CN a unique selling point that it could use to win riders away from competitor Canadian Pacific. Within a few years CN ads would boast that "eleven Canadian National radio stations broadcast from coast to coast." Eventually, this service was transformed into the Canadian Broadcasting Corporation.

In 1927 three new trains were inaugurated. The *Confederation* between Toronto and Vancouver supplemented the *Continental Limited,* which ran between Montreal and Vancouver. The *Confederation* featured a radio-equipped compartment-observation-library buffet car, as well as sleepers, coaches, and a dining car. The Chicago–Toronto–Montreal *Maple Leaf* augmented the existing *International Limited* on the same route, giving travelers a choice of morning or evening

departures from Chicago. Between Montreal and Halifax, where the *Ocean Limited* had been operating since 1904, a second summer-only train, the *Acadian,* began service in June 1927. It offered a radio-equipped compartment-observation-sleeping car.

Too Much Railway, Too Little Traffic

Thornton was an optimist by nature. He inherited a system that was overbuilt for the population and economy it served, but he believed that through aggressive efforts on CN's part to support government immigration policies, the population of the prairie provinces could be increased. With more farmers, there would be more traffic for the railway to carry. According to Donald MacKay, in the mid-1920s CN had 400 field agents whose job was to look for settlement locations and assist immigrants in moving to the prairies. As a result of their efforts, CN settled 4,200 families between 1926 and 1930. Spartan sleeping cars known as "colonist cars" were operated on transcontinental trains to provide settlers with an affordable means of reaching their new homes.

Given the overbuilding of the rail network that had taken place before World War I, and

Engineer L. L. Wood in the cab of Northern No. 6154 in January 1943. *Nicholas Morant/National Film Board of Canada. Photothèque/National Archives of Canada/PA-153050*

the role this played in the financial disintegration of CN's predecessors, one might have expected railway executives of the 1920s to avoid any further construction of rail lines. However, there was still territory that was not served by the rail network. Spurred by its rivalry with Canadian Pacific, CN built 1,895 miles (3,051 kilometers) of new branchlines in the 1920s. According to MacKay, some of these lines "were of questionable value even then in the days before trucking." Between them, he writes, CN and CP "increased Canadian railway mileage by almost one-third in a decade."

Despite the building of new branchlines of marginal economic worth, CN's financial results were improving. In 1929, the company had an operating ratio of 82.5 percent, meaning that roughly 17.5 cents of every dollar that came in from customers was available to cover the cost of CN's debt. Unfortunately, because of the massive financial obligations that the railway had inherited from its predecessors, and the additional debt taken on to fund CN's capital improvements since 1923, this was not enough. The government had to make up the difference. Still, Thornton had brought the operating ratio down significantly in the prior six years. Also, thanks in part to the significant investments in new equipment CN made during the 1920s, the public perception of the government railway had changed dramatically for the better.

John W. Barriger, then president of the Monon Railroad, said in 1944 that during the period from 1920 to 1929, Thornton "was backed by a generous, friendly, and cooperative Government. Parliament approved all of the drafts upon the Dominion treasury for capital expenditures, of every description, which the Canadian National's President recommended were required for the improvement and extension of this railroad."

It did not take long for the collapse of the stock market in October 1929, and the ensuing depression, to undo most of the financial progress CN had made since its formation. By the end of 1930, MacKay notes, "freight traffic had sunk to the lowest level in a decade and passenger travel was the lightest in twenty years." Grain prices fell "to the lowest level in memory. Two hundred thousand Canadians had lost their jobs" by the time of the 1930 general election. CN's operating ratio increased to 88.1 for the year 1930.

The Niagara, St. Catharines & Toronto Railway became a CN subsidiary, along with four other electric lines, in 1923, but kept its own identity until 1958. Car 620, shown here in 1959, was built by Ottawa Car in 1930 and had been operated by another CN electric line, Montreal & Southern Counties, before being transferred to NStC&T in 1956. *Richard Jay Solomon*

The election brought the Conservative party into power. Thornton had done a respectable job of walking the line between the demands of a business and those of a government agency, but some of the excesses that had occurred on his watch made him an easy target for political sniping. The competition with CP had gone to irrational lengths, including the building of unnecessary hotels and ships. CP used its status as a privately owned company, free from political interference, as a platform from which it called for the two railways to be unified.

In November 1931 the Conservative prime minister, R. B. Bennett, appointed a Royal Commission on Railways and Transportation. When it issued its report 10 months later, it took both railways to task for wasteful competition. By then Thornton had resigned effective August 1, 1932. His vice president of operations, maintenance, and construction, Samuel J. Hungerford, was appointed to succeed him. Hungerford had begun his railway career with CP as an apprentice machinist and had joined Canadian Northern in 1910.

The general economic situation was aggravated by drought in both Canada and the United States. Canadian grain production fell by more than two-thirds between 1929 and 1932, and the price of grain dropped even more.

Belt-tightening at CN had already begun before Hungerford was named president. In 1931 two of the passenger trains announced with much fanfare only four years earlier, the *Confederation* and the *Acadian,* were discontinued. Wages were cut and service was curtailed.

In 1933 CN was reorganized, with the semi-independent board of directors replaced by three government-appointed trustees. Job cuts began at the top and extended throughout the company. G. R. Stevens notes that 11 of the top officers appointed by Thornton resigned. Over three years the

total payroll at CN was reduced from 111,389 employees to 70,525.

Although the Royal Commission had rejected a merger of CN and CP, political leverage was used to force cooperation between the two. In the 1920s the only two significant examples of cooperation between the two rivals were in Toronto, where they opened a new Union Station in 1927, and in Alberta, where they took over four provincially owned railways in 1929, renaming them Northern Alberta Railways.

One of the few cooperative efforts to emerge in the early 1930s was a 1933 agreement to pool the two railways' passenger services between Toronto, Ottawa, Montreal, and Quebec City. They also worked together as owners of a fledgling airline, Canadian Airways, which had been built up from a small, privately operated firm. CP's role in the airline was eventually eliminated through parliamentary action, and CN became sole owner of the renamed Trans-Canada Air Lines. Later, the airline would become known as Air Canada.

In 1935 the Liberal party and William Lyon Mackenzie King returned to power. Stevens writes that for CN, "by 1935, the times were on the mend, and the hard climb back to normalcy had begun." Under the King administration, CN management, which had been pleading for years to have the debt on the company's books reduced, got a receptive hearing. The government decided to write off the $1.174 billion in government debt on the company's balance sheet. This left it with $1.185 billion in private debt that the company had inherited from its predecessors. In 1936 another CN responsibility was eliminated when the last nine ships in Canada's merchant marine fleet were sold.

CN Goes to War

In December 1939 CN got an early taste of what would be expected of it during World War II. The Canadian 1st Division was

NOVEMBER 2, 1941

GRAND TRUNK RAILWAY SYSTEM

IN CONNECTION WITH
CANADIAN NATIONAL RAILWAYS

NOVEMBER 2, 1941

CANADIAN NATIONAL RAILWAYS

IN CONNECTION WITH
GRAND TRUNK RAILWAY SYSTEM

A Complete Transport System

FREIGHT

CNR

EXPRESS

Grand Trunk — Canadian National caters to its patrons with excellent

PASSENGER
FREIGHT
EXPRESS
TELEGRAPH
HOTEL
STEAMSHIP
and AIR LINES services

TABLE OF PRINCIPAL CONTENTS PAGE I

INDEX TO STATIONS -- PAGES 73-79
FOLDER B No 109

ordered to embark for Europe through the port of Halifax. According to Donald MacKay, 25 CN trains were used for the movement in a period of 48 hours.

Another early movement through Halifax was in the other direction, and it involved the transfer of $7.5 billion in gold and securities from the Bank of England to more secure facilities in Ottawa and Montreal. MacKay notes that CN trains carrying these valuables were timed to arrive in the early-morning hours so that transfer to

Canadian vaults could be accomplished under cover of darkness.

As CN geared up for the war effort, it made a change in the executive ranks. In July 1941 Hungerford retired and R. C. Vaughan became president. He had previously served as CN's vice president of purchasing and stores.

The war put a strain on several of CN's critical routes, most notably Halifax–Moncton. It took as many as 700 boxcars to

CN took every opportunity to promote awareness of the broad range of services that it offered, as shown by this 1941 timetable. *Author collection*

CN enginehouse employees wipe down an engine at Edmonton in January 1943. During World War II women were hired for jobs that had traditionally been closed to them, although the "running trades" (engineer, conductor, and brakeman) remained male-only for many years after the war. *Nicholas Morant/National Film Board of Canada. Photothèque/National Archives of Canada/C-079524*

fill up a ship being loaded at Halifax, and the port city lacked the yard capacity to allow for an orderly flow of cars prior to each ship. Moncton became a key staging point for this traffic, and on the route between there and Halifax, Centralized Traffic Control (CTC) was installed starting in 1941 to increase line capacity and ensure safe operations.

With an abundance of wartime traffic, and with every employee being worked to his or her maximum, CN's operating efficiency reached new levels. In 1943 its operating ratio was 73.6 percent, a level it would not see again for more than 50 years. By the time 1944 came to an end, 20,165 CN employees had entered military or merchant marine service, and 582 had lost their lives in the war. Several hundred women were employed in jobs that had previously been restricted to men (although the ranks of

CN 6207, shown here at Brockville, Ontario, in August 1958, was built by Montreal Locomotive Works and delivered in July 1942. *Jim Shaughnessy*

CN 4207 at Bridge Station, Quebec, near the former National Transcontinental Bridge crossing the St. Lawrence River in November 1955. This engine was one of a group of ten 2-10-2 Santa Fe-type locomotives that CN acquired from the Boston & Albany Railroad in 1928. *Jim Shaughnessy*

engineers, conductors, and trainmen were still male only).

During the war some projects that had been in the works for years finally came to fruition. Two of these were in Montreal. In 1943 a new Central Station that had been in development since 1929 opened at the south end of the tunnel under Mount Royal. The former GTR Bonaventure station, which had served as CN's main passenger terminal in Montreal, was restricted to Lakeshore commuter trains and troop movements for the balance of the war and then converted to a CN Express freight terminal.

Another long-planned improvement was a connection between CN's yards east and west of downtown Montreal. The former GTR yard at Turcot was CN's main

freight terminal in the city, but there was no direct connection to rail-served industries at the eastern end of the island. Freight between the two zones required a 108-mile (174-kilometer) detour via Joliette and Fresnière Junction, Quebec. To solve this, a 14.3-mile (23.0-kilometer) cutoff was opened in 1945.

When World War II ended, CN had posted an enviable record of service. In both 1943 and 1944 the railway generated more than 36 billion revenue ton-miles (RTMs)—i.e., one ton moved one mile, compared with 17 billion RTMs in 1939. The increase in passenger traffic was even more dramatic: CN recorded 3.6 billion passenger miles in 1943, and slightly more in 1944, versus 875 million in 1939.

But as with World War I, the return to peacetime was a mixed blessing. Cost inflation began to put a squeeze on the company's financial results, and both freight and passenger revenues were drained away by the highway system.

CN's Steam Locomotives

Following the absorption of GTR, CN's roster included 3,265 locomotives, 3,363 passenger cars, and 124,648 freight cars. Some new equipment had already arrived to replace the worn-out cars and locomotives of CN's predecessor railroads. Under the management of D. B. Hanna, the government railway had received 163 new locomotives, 200 passenger cars, and 8,450 freight cars. But this made only a small improvement in the quality of the new railway's fleet, given its vast size.

Over the next several years the average age of CN's fleet dropped as old equipment was scrapped and replaced. In 1923 58 engines were retired, and 420 additional loco-

In 1929 Montreal Locomotive Works delivered 20 Northerns to CN, numbered 6140 through 6159. Here, one of these locomotives is shown under construction. *National Archives of Canada/PA-041340*

Northern 6126, shown here at Toronto, was delivered to CN in 1927. *National Archives of Canada/PA-146823*

motives met the same fate over the next four years. CN replaced obsolete engines with 2-8-2 Mikados, 4-8-2 Mountains, 4-8-4 Northerns (also known as Confederations to mark the sixtieth anniversary of Canada's unification), and 2-10-2 Santa Fe types.

By the time Henry Thornton came on board in 1922, the company already had 225 relatively new Mikados, all delivered since 1916. In 1923 and 1924 an additional 75 of the 2-8-2 type arrived. The final group of five arrived in 1936.

Another early locomotive order was for 16 of the Mountain types, numbered 6000 through 6015 and delivered in 1923. By 1930 an additional 38 Mountains had been delivered. These 4-8-2s featured automatic stokers, superheaters, and all-weather cabs. A final group of 20 semi-streamlined Mountains, numbered 6060 through 6079 and easily identified by their conical noses, was delivered in 1944.

During the Thornton years the Northern represented another key steam locomotive development for CN. The 4-8-4 Northern was as close to a universal locomotive as anything on the CN roster. Deliveries started in 1927, and by 1929 CN had 60 of the engines, numbered 6100 through 6159. Grand Trunk Western (GTW), CN's U.S. subsidiary serving Michigan, Indiana, and Illinois, owned an additional 12, numbered 6300 through 6311. Northerns and Mountains were used in both freight and passenger service, and they were equally at home on the mainline and on secondary routes.

From 1924 through 1930 CN added 48 Santa Fe types (for freight service), five 4-6-4 Hudson locomotives (for fast passenger trains between Montreal and Toronto), and a number of smaller locomotives (notably 0-8-0 yard engines and 2-8-0 Consolidations) to its roster. Locomotive deliveries dried up in the early 1930s, but in 1936 CN added a few

CN's dual-service 4-8-2 Mountains and 4-8-4 Northerns combined pulling power with the ability to negotiate light rail on branchlines. CN 6007 was among the first group of Mountains delivered to CN in 1923. It is shown here at Stratford, Ontario, in February 1959. *Jim Shaughnessy*

more engines to its roster, including 10 Northerns. Five of them, numbered 6400 through 6404, were streamlined, built to a joint design of the railway and the National Research Council. The intent was to keep smoke away from the cab. While they were not successful in meeting that objective, these five photogenic engines were much in demand for special trains.

CN added another 25 Northerns in 1940, 35 more in 1943, and the final group of 30 in 1944. By the end of 1944, CN had

CN 6218 crosses the Richelieu River, approximately 20 miles (32 kilometers) east of Montreal on the St. Hyacinthe Subdivision, in February 1970. The 6218 was used on dozens of excursions following the end of regular CN steam locomotive operation in 1960. It continued in service until 1971. *Jim Shaughnessy*

203 Northerns (more than any other road) and 78 Mountains. The best-known CN Northern, No. 6218, which operated on dozens of fan trips after regular steam operations had ceased, was a member of the class of 1943. Following its retirement, CN 6218 was replaced in excursion service by Mountain 6060.

Early Experiments with the Diesel

One irony of diesel-electric locomotive development in North America is that CN was a pioneer in experimenting with diesel propulsion, yet lagged behind virtually every major U.S. railroad in adopting the new form of motive power for regular operations.

However, even before it acquired its first diesel, CN experimented with other forms of internal combustion, most notably self-propelled passenger cars, which permitted cost savings on branchline runs. One such car could replace a steam locomotive, baggage car, and coach. The operating unions also permitted smaller crews on these cars than on regular trains.

CN historian J. Norman Lowe notes that "the first record of a self-propelled car operating on a CN predecessor line dates back to 1912" on CNoR. By 1926, he says, "CN had 36 self-propelled cars for passenger service. These comprised two steam cars, 10 storage battery units, three gas-electric cars, seven

CN 15709 was a diesel-electric self-propelled car built in 1930, rebuilt at Montreal's Point St. Charles shops in 1951, and converted in 1964 for use in maintaining the suburban electrification north of Montreal. At the time of this photo Suburban electrification was the task of the CN 15709 and trailer No. 15708. The car was replaced by a truck in 1970 and scrapped in 1972. *Jim Shaughnessy*

The twin units of pioneer diesel-electric locomotive No. 9000 were built at the Canadian Locomotive Company shop in Kingston, Ontario, in 1929. Here, one of the units has its 1,330-horsepower, Scottish-built Beardmore engine installed. The units were subsequently separated and operated as CN 9000 and 9001. *Canada Science and Technology Museum, CSTM/CN collection neg. no. 30664*

oil-electric cars with four-cylinder engines, two oil-electric articulated units with eight-cylinder engines, 10 gasoline units and two multiple-unit electrics." Clearly, this was a time of experimentation.

In 1929 a two-unit diesel, built at Canadian Locomotive Company's (CLC) Kingston, Ontario, shop, began its career on CN. CN No. 9000 (which became two separate units, 9000 and 9001, in 1931) had a 12-cylinder, 1,330-horsepower Beardmore diesel engine in each unit. CN 9000 was the brainchild of CN's chief of motive power, C. E. (Ned) Brooks. After a series of test runs, including one to Vancouver, this pioneer diesel was put into revenue service on passenger trains between Toronto and Montreal.

The twin units, 9000 and 9001, were withdrawn from revenue service in 1939, but number 9000 had a second life during World War II as part of an armored train designed to protect the Prince Rupert line. It saw revenue service between Moncton and Quebec City in 1945, but both units were scrapped in 1946.

CN also fielded two other early diesels, CN No. 7700 (later CN 77), built in 1929 at CLC, and Grand Trunk Western No. 7730 (later GTW 73), a Brill product built in 1926. However, with the premature death of Ned Brooks in 1933 at age 46, the diesel locomotive lost its most ardent sponsor at CN. It would be 1948 before CN bought another diesel locomotive for road service.

CN 7750 was one of the company's pioneer diesel-electric locomotives. Constructed in 1932 at the Point St. Charles shops in Montreal, it survived until 1948, when it was heavily damaged in a collision in the Mount Royal Tunnel. *National Archives of Canada/PA-164829*

During its years as a government-owned railway, CN had limited freedom to abandon trackage and so was forced to continue operating many lines that had light traffic and light rail. The RSC13, with its A1A-A1A axle arrangement, was one way that CN dealt with this dilemma. CN 1729, 1701, and 1718 are seen here at Opleman, Prince Edward Island (near O'Leary station) in May 1975. This train consisted of empty potato reefers and supplies for the Canadian Forces base at Summerside, P.E.I. *Phil Mason*

CHAPTER THREE

POSTWAR CN:
Years of Modernization and Growth

World War II left Canadian National in much the same situation as World War I: physically worn out and faced with rampant cost inflation. Between 1944 and 1948 operating expenses increased 28 percent, but revenues rose only 11 percent. As a regulated company CN could not simply raise freight rates to offset its higher costs. If the company was going to survive, it had to become more efficient, so that it could keep more of every dollar it took in.

Dieselization

The most obvious route to efficiency was one that was already well under way in the United States: converting from steam locomotives to diesel-electrics. Steam locomotives were high-maintenance machines. Their operating range was limited because they needed frequent watering and fueling. They had to be turned at the end of their runs. Each steam locomotive required an engineer and fireman. In terms of economics, the diesel was clearly superior to steam.

Although it had pioneered the use of diesel locomotives in mainline service, CN had since been surpassed by U.S. railroads. By January 1948 the company (including its U.S. subsidiaries) had 75 diesels in yard service, but no diesel road locomotives.

That year the dieselization process moved ahead in a small way with the purchase of 28 F3 units from General Motors' Electro-Motive Division for mainline service (six for CN and 22 for GTW). CN also acquired several 650-horsepower units built by Whitcomb Locomotive Works (a U.S. manufacturer of mining and industrial locomotives) and CLC for use on Prince Edward Island. Why P.E.I.? First, it was small. Any issues that needed to be addressed would be local ones, and wouldn't affect the rest of the CN system. Second, operating steam engines on the island was expensive because coal had to be brought in by ship from Nova Scotia. The Prince Edward Island pilot project wasn't an immediate success (the Whitcomb units were rejected as mechanically unfit for service and replaced with 18 similar

In August 1962 the morning eastbound train from Summerside pulls into a Hunter River stop en route to Charlottetown. Prince Edward Island was the first region of CN to be dieselized, and Nos. 28 and 25 were among a group of 18 General Electric 70-tonners that CN acquired for this purpose in 1950. *Jim Shaughnessy*

units from General Electric), however, CN was moving in the right direction.

Full-scale dieselization would have to wait for the arrival of a fresh face in CN corporate headquarters. Donald Gordon was a Scotsman by birth and banker by trade who moved to CN from the Bank of Canada in December 1949. At 47 he was the youngest person to hold the title of president at CN, and the first non-railroader. He took over a company that was struggling financially. CN recorded a deficit of $42 million in 1949. It was what would be called in later years a "multi-modal" company, operating a fleet of coastal and ocean-going ships, trucks to serve its express customers, and buses that connected with its passenger trains. It also owned Trans-Canada Air Lines. But the heart of the business was the railway, and it was this part of the business that got most of Gordon's attention.

Even to a non-railroader it was clear that CN's equipment fleet needed to be rejuvenated. Donald MacKay, in his book *The People's Railway*, tells the story of a vice president who asked for authority to buy 1,000 boxcars but was told by Gordon to increase the order to 5,000. He believed that if CN was to be taken seriously by its customers, it had to offer them modern equipment, both freight and passenger.

Three of the GE 70-tonners that dieselized Prince Edward Island team up on the westbound freight from Souris to Charlottetown at Mt. Stewart Junction in May 1975. *Phil Mason*

CN 8702 was among the railroad's earliest road diesel locomotives, having been built in 1952 by Canadian Locomotive Company. Here the unit leads a freight train at Ballantyne, Quebec, outside Montreal, in November 1955. *Jim Shaughnessy*

The extent of the job that lay ahead in the motive power department is indicated in a December 31, 1951, summary of CN's locomotive fleet. On that date CN (excluding its U.S. subsidiaries) had 68 road diesels, 30 road switchers, and 120 diesel yard engines. But these diesels made up only 7 percent of the CN fleet's total tractive power. At the time CN rostered 2,226 steam locomotives, many of them coal-fired. Three out of every four were more than 30 years old. Among the antiquities in this fleet were 198 4-6-0 Ten-Wheelers, 34 2-6-0 Moguls, and 249 0-6-0

switchers. The most powerful steam locomotives in the fleet were 93 2-10-2 Santa Fe types, followed by 179 4-8-4 Northerns.

CN dieselized on a terminal-by-terminal and region-by-region basis, which allowed operating and mechanical personnel on each part of the railway to learn about the new machines. But by mid-1952, aside from P.E.I., only one region had been converted: Quebec's Gaspé Peninsula, where a fleet of 15 1,200-horsepower road switchers built by CLC to a Fairbanks-Morse design had superseded steam. Diesels were also operating on selected long-distance freight trains out of Montreal, but they were working side-by-side with steam. On the passenger side, steam still ruled.

Despite the preponderance of steam engines on CN's roster, diesels were hauling an increasing share of the company's trains. In 1952 diesels generated 23 percent of the railway's gross ton-miles. By the end of that year the company had 58 F7A and 18 F7B units, representing its first significant group of road-freight diesels. These were in addition to the four F3As and two F3Bs for CN, and 22 F3A units for Grand Trunk Western, delivered in 1948. The F3 units, like CN's early General Motors (GM) switchers, were built by GM's Electro-Motive Division (EMD) at its LaGrange, Illinois, plant. In 1950, GM set up a Canadian locomotive assembly plant at London, Ontario which became known as General Motors Diesel Division (GMD). From 1950 to 1988, CN's U.S. subsidiaries received their GM products from EMD, while GM diesels for CN itself were built by GMD at London. In 1988 GM consolidated North American locomotive assembly operations at London.

Some of the notable deliveries over the next few years included:
• 1953 and 1954: 41 RS3 units built by Montreal Locomotive Works (MLW). Over the period 1955 through 1960, these road switchers would be followed by 51 1,600-horsepower RS10 units and 225 1,800-horsepower RS18 units from MLW.
• 1954: 17 GP9 units from EMD for Grand

CN 7603 was built by Canadian Locomotive Company to a Fairbanks-Morse design, with an A1A-A1A axle configuration. Here it makes a station stop at Cross Point, 12.8 miles (20.6 kilometers) east of Matapédia, Quebec, in January 1952. *Canada Science and Technology Museum, CSTM/CN collection neg. no. 47702*

CN had one H24-66 Trainmaster. It was built at Beloit, Wisconsin, by Fairbanks-Morse and delivered to CN in 1955 as CN No. 3000. The following year it was renumbered CN 2900. Here it handles a cut of ore cars at Port Arthur, Ontario, in 1956. *Canada Science and Technology Museum, CSTM/CN collection neg. no. X42527*

Trunk Western (2 for passenger service and 15 for freight). These were the first of what would become the CN family's 434 GP9s (349 on CN, 57 on GTW, and 28 on Central Vermont), the largest fleet of this locomotive model in North America.

• 1954 and 1955: 14 FP9A and 14 F9B units from GMD to power the new *Super Continental,* followed by 29 additional FP9A and 24 more F9B units in 1957 and 1958.

In April 1960 CN retired its last steam locomotive from regular service. By the end of that year it had 2,134 diesel locomotives in service.

Technology: CTC and the Computer

The 1950s were clearly the decade of dieselization on CN, but that was not all that was being done to modernize the railway. Centralized Traffic Control (CTC), which

offered improved safety, higher line capacity, and lower operating costs, was also spreading. It combined elements of Automatic Block Signaling (ABS) which CN already had in place on many of its busiest routes, with remote control of switches and signals by an operator or train dispatcher.

The first CTC installation on CN had been between Halifax and Moncton, 185 miles (298 kilometers), during World War II. In 1949 the second mainline segment of CTC was completed, between West Junction and Ste. Rosalie on the Drummondville Subdivision, giving CN a total of 301 miles (485 kilometers) of CTC.

New CTC installations continued over the next decade, and by the end of 1960 CN had CTC on 2,039 miles (3,283 kilometers) of its mainline. Over the next four years an additional 1,336 miles (2,151 kilometers) of

CTC were installed. Most of the CTC installed in the 1950s and early 1960s was what CN called "modified" CTC, which had a power switch at only one end of each controlled siding, as opposed to conventional CTC, which has a power switch at both ends. This meant that the train approaching the power switch would always take the siding, and then exit through a spring switch at the other end. It was not a perfect solution, but it was a big advance over the timetable-and-train order system that had preceded it. Eventually, CN would upgrade to a full CTC system on its mainlines as traffic growth in the 1970s forced it to extend sidings and take other measures to increase line capacity.

CN was making progress on other fronts as well. In 1960 it opened its first modern classification yard at Moncton, to be followed by other automatically controlled hump yards at Edmonton, Winnipeg, Montreal, and Toronto. It was also beginning to use radio for field operations, first in yards, and then for end-to-end train communication on the road.

The single technological advance of the 1960s and 1970s that most changed the way railroading had been practiced for decades was the computer. Electronic data systems were first used in the rail industry for payroll and other accounting functions, where batch processing could be used to simplify tasks that had once taken rooms full of clerks to perform. What changed starting in the late

Montreal Locomotive Works built diesel locomotives under a partnership with U.S. builder Alco, and many of its models had Alco counterparts. RS18 No. 3115, shown here at Toronto in 1962, is identical, except cosmetically, to the RS11 model produced by Alco in the United States. *Collection of George Carpenter*

Between 1954 and 1958 CN acquired 43 FP9A units and 38 F9B units to power its prestige transcontinental trains. CN 6539 is shown here at North Bay, Ontario. *Richard Jay Solomon*

CN's C-Liners did not have long life spans compared with the steam locomotives they replaced, many of which served for 30 years or more. CN 9328 (shown here at North Bay, Ontario, in May 1966) was delivered in early 1953 by Canadian Locomotive Company, and retired in 1966. *P. D. Custer Jr. Collection of George Carpenter*

1960s was an increasing use of computers for "real-time" functions. In 1961 and 1962 CN installed new computers at its Montreal headquarters and at several key points around the system to help handle car tracing, revenue accounting, and equipment control. This involved sending data on a magnetic tape to the master computer in Montreal—clearly not a real-time application.

In 1967 CN began to develop a Traffic Reporting and Control System (TRACS) that allowed for timely reporting of train arrivals and departures, car locations, and other information critical for the operation of the railway. This made CN less dependent on local station and yard personnel for recording car locations and movements. In 1970 CN established eight "Servocentres" that were, in essence, centralized freight billing and customer service units. Increasing centralization of clerical functions would continue for the next two decades.

New computer systems did more than reduce the labor intensity and timeliness of data collection, however. Car distribution was an early beneficiary of improvements in information technology. For many years empty cars would be sent to stations on the basis of past loading patterns. Now CN could respond quickly to specific customer requirements. In 1977 CN credited TRACS with a 10 percent improvement in car utilization, which it said was "equivalent to a saving of about $30 million a year."

Growing to Serve the Canadian Economy

CN needed all the help it could get from the diesel locomotive, CTC, computers, and other forms of technology. In 1943, the peak traffic year of World War II, it had generated 36.3 billion revenue ton-miles (RTMs). Despite the falloff in business immediately after the war, by the mid-1950s the railway was setting new traffic records. In 1956 CN achieved a temporary record of 41.9 billion RTMs, but by 1964 that record, too, had been eclipsed. After 1964, traffic grew almost every year. In 1973 CN generated 72.4 billion RTMs, almost double the World War II peak. And it was doing so with about 13 percent fewer employees than it had during the war.

Bulk traffic was growing, and, in response, CN began to operate unit trains that kept cars together from origin to destination and back again, in a continuous cycle that would be interrupted only for car maintenance. In 1968 CN began operating what it called "the first predesigned unit train in Canada," carrying pelletized ore from a mine near Temagami in northern Ontario to Hamilton on a 72-hour cycle. Unit trains reduced costs for the railway and made service more predictable for shippers. Most of them included an empty movement back to origin, but CN came up with one unit train operating plan that shipped potash westbound to Vancouver and a return movement of phosphate rock to fertilizer plants near Edmonton.

CN 1299 was part of a fleet of 187 CN units of model SW1200RS. They were equipped with Flexicoil trucks and large numberboard/headlight assemblies so that they could be used in road service on branchlines. No. 1299 is shown at Turcot Yard, Montreal, in May 1958. *Richard Jay Solomon*

CN extra 5403 west carries export sulfur through Yellowhead Pass, Alberta, in October 1989, en route to the port of Vancouver. The growth of such bulk commodities in the 1980s put a strain on CN's western network, and the company invested millions of dollars in siding extensions, signal system improvements and other capacity enhancements. *Steve Patterson*

Another source of growth was intermodal traffic trailers on flatcars (TOFC, or "piggyback"), and, in the 1960s, containers on flatcars (COFC, mainly for international traffic). CN got into the intermodal business in December 1952 when it began moving trailers on overnight trains between Toronto and Montreal. Over the next several years piggyback service was extended to locations large and small in eastern Canada. In 1959 TOFC facilities opened in Regina, Calgary, Edmonton, and Vancouver. The young intermodal business grew much faster than the rest of CN's traffic. By the early 1960s CN began to invest in modern handling facilities at larger terminals to reduce the cost and improve the timeliness of loading and unloading. In 1964, the company reported that piggyback volumes had grown 30.9 percent over the previous year, with revenues increasing 27.3 percent. In 1967 CN established rates specifically for container movements between East Coast ports (Halifax, Saint John, and Montreal) and interior Canadian points. In 1971 a new container terminal opened at Halifax. That year the company handled more than 90,000 import-export containers. By 1974 that number had grown to 166,000.

In the early days of piggyback service, before volumes justified dedicated intermodal trains, it was common to see a few trailers on the rear of a manifest freight. These trailers are at Cote de Noir, Quebec, en route to Quebec City, in 1962. *Canada Science and Technology Museum, CSTM/CN collection neg. no. 55565.1*

The Economics of a National Railway: People or Profits?

CN was led during these years by Norman MacMillan, a CN veteran who had succeeded Donald Gordon as president in January 1967. The MacMillan years were ones not only of growth for CN, but also of an increasingly commercial business philosophy for the railway. His move to the president's office coincided with the passage of the National Transportation Act, which eased the regulatory environment in Canada a full 13 years before such changes would occur in the United States. This made it easier for Canadian railways to implement services geared to the needs of specific customers and to abandon money-losing operations.

MacMillan, who retired as chief executive officer in 1974, had hoped to see CN turn a profit during his tenure. While it made good progress in that direction, the company continued to run yearly operating deficits until 1976. By that time Robert Bandeen, a 43-year-old Ph.D. economist and a graduate of CN's research-and-development department who had also run its U.S. subsidiaries for a time, had succeeded MacMillan. He reorganized CN into "profit centres" to quantify the financial contribution (or loss) of each CN operating unit. In the words of Donald MacKay, Bandeen "made CN more entrepreneurial . . . . He set out to end the deficits in what was, technologically, one of the best railways in North America."

In 1976 the company recorded its first operating profit in two decades. CN Rail, as the Canadian freight operation was designated, generated income of $157 million, an improvement over the $23 million in income for 1975, and enough to offset money-losing operations in express, passenger, and hotel services. Income at CN's U.S. rail unit, Grand Trunk Corporation (which included Grand Trunk Western Railroad; Central Vermont Railway; and Duluth, Winnipeg & Pacific Railway) went from $3.5 million in

1975 to $13.9 million in 1976. These figures were a bit misleading, because they did not take into account the fact that CN continued to struggle under a huge debt burden, but they did represent a milestone in the evolution of the company from a government agency to a free-enterprise corporation.

In CN's annual report for 1976, management noted that the financial improvement was the result of "stringent cost control, alert marketing, and benefits from past technological advances." The report went on, "while

earning a profit in 1976, CN continued to fulfill its mandate of service to its owners—the people of Canada." But what did its owners really want—a profitable corporation or an organization that would provide social benefits in the form of jobs and services?

Most of the big issues that Robert Bandeen would grapple with over the next few years involved, in one way or another, the question of whether CN could become financially self-sustaining. The issues included the following:

Insulating CN from the continuing cash drain of the passenger business. In 1977 a new CN subsidiary, VIA Rail Canada, was established to take over the operation of both CN and CP passenger trains. The following year the company became a separate government-established corporation (a "crown corporation" in Canadian parlance), thus eliminating this financial drain on CN.

Financial losses in the Atlantic provinces. In 1979 CN formed a subsidiary, TerraTransport, to operate rail, intermodal,

The last surviving Grand Trunk Western F3, No. 9013, was transferred to CN in 1972 for an F7 rebuilding program. It reemerged in 1973 as CN No. 9171, shown here as the trailing unit on a CN locomotive consist at Kitwanga, British Columbia, in October 1978. *Stan Smaill*

CN 5082 is eastbound at Cisco, British Columbia, in June 1975 with covered hoppers returning from the port of Vancouver. Power for this train is a set of three General Motors Diesel Division SD40 units. *Steve Patterson*

In 1973 CN received 30 M420(W) locomotives, the first with the redesigned "comfort cab" from Montreal Locomotive Works. CN 2551, seen here at Rouses Point, New York, in July 1975, is from a second M420(W) order, delivered the following year. *Tom Murray*

In 1975 CN converted 38 RS18 locomotives, built with a B-B axle arrangement, to an A1A-A1A configuration. During the rebuilding, the units were de-rated from 1,800 to 1,400 horsepower, and when completed they were given model designation RSC14. CN 1753 and 1750, shown here at Hunter Island, Prince Edward Island, in August 1984, were part of that group. *Steve Patterson*

CN was never reluctant to order innovative, unconventional, or unique locomotives. One of its innovations was the "Draper taper." CN wanted a full-width (or "cowl") body for its locomotives to allow for engine compartment access with some protection from the elements. The drawback was that such a design had limited visibility from the cab toward the rear. CN's assistant chief of motive power, William Draper, solved the problem with a slight narrowing of the cowl, a design first used on a 1985 order. Here the headlight of a passing train shows the Draper taper on SD50F No. 5403 at Henry House, Alberta, in October 1989. *Steve Patterson*

"In 1978, there was a major move to segregate rail and non-rail operations. CN Rail assumed responsibility for all continental rail and intermodal operations. CN Holdings [of which Mr. Armstrong became president] assumed responsibility for Trucking, Hotels, CN Tower, Telecommunications, Express, Marine, Newfoundland, Drydocks, and Real Estate with a mandate to promote stand-alone enterprises. An additional venture, Explorations, was subsequently added to exploit corporate gas and oil interests. This proved a well-planned tactic that facilitated the later disposal of non-core assets and the transfer of the real estate portfolio to the Government as part of the [1995] privatization package."

Some of the new business ventures during the Bandeen years made use of existing CN assets, like its oil and gas exploration unit, which was focused on land that CN had inherited from Canadian Northern. Other ventures took CN into businesses that, while related to the railway, were seen by some as distractions from CN's core business. One of these ventures was CN's 1975 investment in the CAST container line. This deal helped put business on the railway, but CN's timing was not good. A North Atlantic rate war hurt CAST's financial performance, and CN ended up writing off its investment in the company in 1982.

Bandeen served as CN's chief executive officer until April 1982. He played a pivotal role not only in modernizing the way the corporation was organized, financed, and operated, but also in framing the conversation with CN's owners—the people of Canada—about what role the company should play in the life of the country.

Opposite: Trains designated as express trains were allowed 5 miles per hour more than ordinary freight trains. No. 212 was so designated. In February 1978 a trio of six-axle Montreal Locomotive Works Century Series locomotives lead that train past the CN depot at St. Hyacinthe, Quebec. During the 1970s these locomotives were the backbone of the mainline fleet east of Montreal. *George Pitarys*

Above: There was a lot of light rail on the prairies, and the A1A-A1A GMD1 from General Motors Diesel was CN's answer to that challenge. It was essentially an SW1200 on a longer frame. GMD built 78 of the six-axle GMD1 units for CN, and five for Northern Alberta Railways. It also built 18 four-axle GMD1 units for CN, which were equipped with steam generators for passenger service. Here No. 1069 is seen at Winnipeg, Manitoba, in May 1976. *Stan Smaill*

Eastbound and westbound *Super Continentals* meet at Lucerne, British Columbia, 4 miles (6 kilometers) west of Yellowhead Pass, in September 1978. *Steve Patterson*

CHAPTER FOUR

CN PASSENGER SERVICE

Canadian National offered a diversity of passenger services and equipment that was arguably as great as that of any North American railroad—a diversity that could often be sampled in the course of a single trip. In 1970, for example, a traveler making his way from Cartierville, Quebec, (in suburban Montreal) to Dewey, British Columbia, (200 miles [322 kilometers] west of Jasper, Alberta) would board a day coach hauled by an electric locomotive. At Central

The *Super Continental* pauses at Armstrong, Ontario, on its journey from Montreal to Vancouver in January 1970. The train has completed 964.4 miles (1,552.0 kilometers) of its 2,914-mile (4,692-kilometer) transcontinental journey. *Tom Murray*

Station, Montreal, he would step onto Train 1, the *Super Continental*, for a 5:05 p.m. departure. He would dine that evening and for the next two days-plus in a dining car built by Pullman-Standard in 1954 as part of CN's program to re-equip its premier long-distance trains. Overnight, he might be booked into the *Evanston,* a sleeping car consisting of four open sections (upper and lower berths with curtains for privacy), four double bedrooms, and eight duplex roomettes, from the same 1954 car order.

At Edmonton a former Milwaukee Road full-length dome car with lounge facilities (known as a Sceneramic car on CN) would be added for the trip through the mountains of western Alberta and British Columbia. At Jasper, the traveler would transfer to Train 9, the tri-weekly train to Prince Rupert, British Columbia, consisting of coaches, dining car, and sleeping car (and generally hauled by a freight locomotive augmented by a steam generator car) for the next 107 miles (172 kilometers) to McBride, British Columbia, where he would arrive at 1:30 a.m. If it was a Sunday night, he might get a room in the McBride Hotel, and at 6:30 a.m. on Tuesday he would depart on a mixed train, No. 297, for the last 92-mile (148-kilometer) lap to his destination. No. 297 would likely have a GP9 up front, a few boxcars, and, on the rear, a combine with a baggage compartment at one end and seating for passengers and crew at the other. If it was winter, then the crew would have the coal stove in the passenger compartment fired up before leaving McBride.

From Streamliners to Mixed Trains, and Everything in Between

The CN timetable of 1970 contained a variety of other trains:

• In addition to the *Super Continental,* transcontinental travelers could ride an unnamed coach-only train (No. 7) from Montreal to Winnipeg (with a connecting train between Capreol, Ontario, and

Toronto) and, after a daylong layover at Winnipeg, board the *Panorama,* which carried sleeping cars as well as coaches from Winnipeg to Vancouver.

• East of Montreal, three trains operated with coaches, sleeping cars, diners, and lounge cars

similar to those on the *Super Continental*: the *Scotian* and the *Ocean* to Halifax (with a section of the *Ocean* being switched out at Truro, Nova Scotia, to continue to Sydney, Nova Scotia), and the *Chaleur* to Gaspé, Quebec.
• Intercity trains, some with club cars, operated in the Montreal–Quebec, Montreal–Toronto, Montreal–Ottawa, and Ottawa–Toronto corridors. In the heavily traveled region between Windsor, London, and Toronto, *Tempo* trains with dedicated equipment provided five schedules daily, augmented by three Railiner (Budd

CN train No. 41 operated between Ottawa and Brockville, Ontario, where it connected with train No. 51, the *Lakeshore,* from Montreal to Toronto. It is shown here making a stop at the Canadian Pacific station in Smiths Falls, Ontario, in September 1971. From here to Brockville, No. 41 will operate on CP via trackage rights. *Tom Murray*

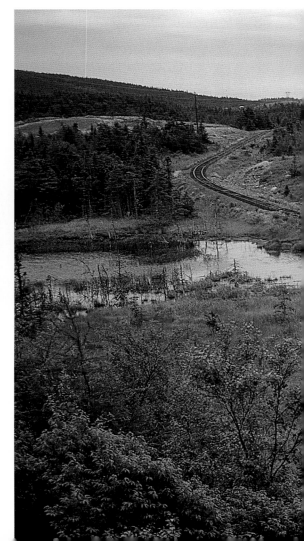

Three days a week, train No. 93 left Winnipeg en route to Churchill, Manitoba, a distance of 976.4 miles (1,571.4 kilometers). On this day in February 1974, the train is ready to depart Winnipeg with freight F7s for power and two steam generator cars for heat. *Tom Murray*

Several routes that had once had passenger trains were listed in the CN timetable, but the conveyances were now buses. This category included the mainline in Newfoundland between St. John's and Port aux Basques; Prince Edward Island; London to St. Thomas, Ontario; and Kamloops to Kelowna, British Columbia. Not included in the CN system timetable, but operated by it, were commuter services in Montreal, Toronto, and Detroit.

Serving All Canada

Canadian National had always made passenger service a priority. In part this was because CN was not strictly a for-profit business, but was an organization intended to serve Canada's broader social and economic needs. In its early years the emphasis on passenger service was influenced by its leader, Sir Henry Thornton, who had spent a substantial part of his pre-CN career running passenger operations in the United States (the Long Island Rail Road) and the United Kingdom (the Great Eastern Railway).

Unlike CP, which was able to look at passenger trains as a business segment (within the constraints set by government regulators), CN was expected to provide service for its own sake. A traditional argument for offering a high-class passenger service was that it would send a positive message to shippers, but CN needed to send a positive message to a wider constituency: the taxpayers and voters who were ultimately responsible for funding the company.

One motto that CN used for many years was "To Everywhere in Canada." Because of the extensive nature of its passenger network,

CN 804 and 805 at Brigus Junction, Newfoundland, in July 1984 on the Carbonear mixed train. *Steve Patterson*

In February 1954 the *Inter-City Limited* with Mountain-type CN 6071 has departed Hamilton, Ontario, and is passing through Bayview Junction en route to Toronto. *Jim Shaughnessy*

CN played an important role in the lives of Canadians. CN trains took immigrants to their new homes on the prairies, brought the necessities of life to remote communities, and carried the mail. Whenever a major change in someone's life occurred—going off to college, joining the military, relocating to a new city—CN was likely to be involved.

Yet CN didn't serve Canadians exclusively. It actively promoted its passenger services to those outside Canada. In 1925,

for example, the company published *Scenic Canada,* a book of photographs taken across Canada and even as far afield as Alaska (CN did, after all, operate coastal vessels in the Pacific). The four pages of text that preceded the photos began with flowery prose: "The route of the Canadian National Railways from the Atlantic to the Pacific lies through a part of the North American continent upon which Nature has been particularly beneficent in the bestowal of gifts that excite

Grand Trunk Western No. 4913 passes through Bayview Junction, Ontario, in August 1957 with a Windsor-bound passenger train. Helper No. 3467 waits on the siding to push westbounds up Dundas Hill. *Jim Shaughnessy*

Hotels of Distinction

The Canadian National system maintains, in some of the principal cities of Canada, hotels which are a credit both to a great transcontinental railway and to the cities served. The Chateau Laurier, (upper left), which stands in the Dominion capital, Ottawa, is one of the finest buildings in Canada and is the centre of the city's most brilliant social life. Other dignified buildings in the Canadian National hotel chain are the Fort Garry, at Winnipeg (left), the Macdonald, at Edmonton (right), and the Nova Scotian, at Halifax (upper right), opened in 1930. In addition to these are: the Prince Arthur, at Port Arthur, Ontario, and the Prince Edward, at Brandon, Manitoba.

Page 22

If CN wanted to fill up its passenger trains, it then had to give passengers some destinations to motivate them to travel. Its hotels, as well as resorts like the Jasper Park Lodge, were part of that strategy, as shown in this excerpt from a 1931 travel brochure. *Author collection*

the admiration and wonder of mankind." By the late 1920s CN had 20 offices in the United States where travelers could book rail, steamship, and hotel reservations, as well as all-inclusive vacation packages.

Jasper Park, with its "sky-piercing mountains, colossal glaciers, torrential rivers, foam-flaked rapids, placid mirror-like lakes, cool deep forests and amid all this a splendid golf course, winding bridle paths and shady nooks," was a centerpiece of CN's advertising. CN owned the Jasper Park Lodge, opened in 1921, and it anchored the Triangle Tour, a staple of CN passenger promotion for decades. The legs of the triangle consisted of rail from Vancouver to Jasper and from Jasper to Prince Rupert, followed by a 600-mile (960-kilometer) cruise from Prince Rupert to Vancouver through the "mountain-guarded Inside Passage of the North Pacific."

CN complemented its passenger trains with hotels at strategic locations across Canada. Between 1912 and 1915 Grand Trunk Railway opened three chateau-style hotels: the Chateau Laurier in Ottawa, the Hotel Fort Garry in Winnipeg, and the Hotel Macdonald in Edmonton. GTR also operated the Minaki Lodge in western Ontario, opened in 1914 and rebuilt by CN following a fire in the 1920s.

From 1928 to 1932 CN opened the Hotel Nova Scotian in Halifax, the Canadian National Hotel (later renamed the Hotel Charlottetown) on Prince Edward Island, and the Bessborough Hotel in Saskatoon. The Hotel Vancouver was started by CN and completed in 1939 in a joint arrangement with CP. The Queen Elizabeth in Montreal, built over Central Station, was opened by CN in 1958. The company's final two hotel ventures were in the Maritimes: the Hotel Beausejour in Moncton, New Brunswick (1972) and a new Hotel Newfoundland in St. John's (1982). In the mid-1980s CN's hotel properties were sold to Canadian Pacific.

The Evolution of CN Passenger Service

Some of the trains operated by CN had long histories. Notable among them were the *International Limited,* which began service in 1900 between Montreal and Chicago on the Grand Trunk, and the *Ocean Limited,* which was inaugurated by the Intercolonial Railway in 1904.

All of CN's predecessors contributed passenger services of their own. Canadian Northern had started a transcontinental service in 1916, using 78 new passenger cars. The trip between Toronto and Vancouver on CNoR's premier train, No. 1 westbound and No. 2 eastbound, took five full days.

Grand Trunk Pacific's prestige train, also numbered 1 and 2, offered "electric lighted standard sleeping cars, containing drawing room, compartment and ten sections, reading lamps in all berths upper and lower," and "meals a la carte," on the three-day journey between Winnipeg and Prince Rupert.

In 1955 CN acquired 12 Fairbanks-Morse-designed, CLC-built passenger units (6 A and 6 B units) in an unusual B-A1A axle configuration. The units spent most of their lives in eastern Canada. Here, CN 6704 prepares to depart from Halifax, Nova Scotia, with the *Ocean Limited* in August 1959. *Jim Shaughnessy*

Following World War II CN found itself with a passenger car fleet badly in need of modernization. It addressed the problem in 1953 when it ordered 218 coaches from Canadian Car & Foundry, and 141 sleeping, dining, and parlor cars from Pullman-Standard. *Author collection*

Opposite: Once it acquired new equipment for the *Super Continental* and its other premier trains, CN improved their operation and promoted them heavily. Inside this 1955 brochure the railway provided photos of sleeping car and coach accommodations and discussed the tightening of the train's schedule by up to 14 hours. *Author collection*

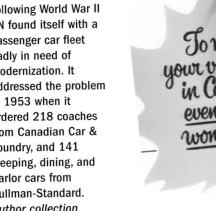

To make your vacation in Canada even more wonderful...

For a between-meal "snack" or moderately priced meal, you'll find that the new and novel dinette cars provide convenient dining service in the modern manner.

Attend the Shakespearean Festival at Stratford, Ont. July-Aug. Visit Canada's romantic Eastern Cities. The walled city of Quebec; Ottawa, Canada's capital; Montreal, "The Paris of North America"; the great city of Toronto.

With three wide, comfortable berths and completely enclosed toilet facilities, Canadian National's modern drawing rooms offer ideal night and day accommodations for family groups.

Canadian National makes RECORD PURCHASE of new passenger equipment!

This record purchase marks the beginning of a new era in Canadian train travel. These modern cars offer a complete choice of accommodations . . . are designed to provide the utmost in comfort, in convenience, in beauty. Every day more of these cars are joining our fleet of famous "name" trains. By midsummer, they will all be in service, helping to make your Canadian National vacation more wonderful than ever.

Deep in Ontario's lovely Lake-of-the-Woods region is Minaki Lodge, a luxurious log-bungalow resort in a delightful lakeland district. Marvellous fishing . . . golf on forest-lined fairways . . . motorboating, canoeing, swimming and tennis. You will have a vacation you'll never forget.

In spacious new C.N.R. coaches you view the changing scenery through wide picture windows . . . stretch out on your reclining foam rubber seat.

Choose one of Canada's 10 Top Maple Leaf Vacations

1. The Scenic Route Across Canada
2. Alaska Cruise via the Inside Passage
3. The Provinces-by-the-Sea
4. Eastern Cities and the Laurentians
5. Sub-Arctic Hudson Bay Tour
6. Romantic French Canada
7. Minaki (Lake of the Woods)
8. Highlands of Ontario
9. British Columbia "Triangle Tour"
10. Jasper in the Canadian Rockies

CANADIAN NATIONAL RAILWAYS

THE ONLY RAILWAY SERVING ALL 10 PROVINCES OF CANADA

Ask about Canada's Top Maple Leaf Vacations or let CANADIAN NATIONAL RAILWAYS experts package a tour for you to include side trips and stopovers. Canadian National offices in principal U.S. cities. In Canada, Passenger Department, 360 McGill St., Montreal. Or see your Travel Agent.

The National Transcontinental operated a name train, the *National,* in conjunction with GTR and the Temiskaming & Northern Ontario Railway (T&NO, predecessor of Ontario Northland) between Toronto and Winnipeg. "Finest Equipment" and "Splendid Roadbed" proclaimed a 1917 timetable listing for this service.

CN did not take long after its creation to knit together the trackage of its predecessors into a through passenger route. The *Continental Limited* was inaugurated on

Announcing Canadian National's New Train

the **SUPER** Continental

FASTER TRANSCONTINENTAL SERVICE

DAILY MONTREAL - OTTAWA - TORONTO - WINNIPEG
SASKATOON - EDMONTON - JASPER - VANCOUVER

COMMENCING APRIL 24th, 1955

✓ convenient inter-city schedules

✓ smart, modern equipment

✓ budget-priced meals

CANADIAN NATIONAL RAILWAYS

DIESELIZED ALL THE WAY!

Train No. 16, the *Chaleur* from Montreal to Gaspé, leaves the mainline at Matapédia, where it will change engine crews, in August 1984. The ex-CN FPA4 locomotive has been repainted to reflect its ownership by VIA Rail Canada. *Steve Patterson*

December 3, 1920 using portions of Grand Trunk, National Transcontinental, Grand Trunk Pacific, and Canadian Northern, as well as the T&NO between North Bay and Cochrane. The route provided a 108-hour schedule from Montreal to Vancouver. Between Kamloops, British Columbia, and Jasper, it carried an open "mountain observation car" that one CN veteran remembers as "an exciting, if somewhat dirty, experience."

The 1920s were a decade of tangible improvements in CN passenger service. A radio service was implemented, and in 1927 new trains were put into service between Toronto and Vancouver (the *Confederation*), Montreal and Chicago (the *Maple Leaf*), and Montreal and Halifax (the *Acadian,* an all-sleeping car train).

The Great Depression brought an end to new service and equipment, and a dramatic reduction in passenger revenues, but throughout the 1930s CN continued to operate a large fleet of passenger trains. A 1936 timetable lists 14 "Important Trains," including the *Continental Limited* between Montreal (and Toronto) and Vancouver; the *International Limited, Maple Leaf,* and *Inter-City Limited* between Montreal, Detroit, and Chicago; the *Washingtonian* and *Montrealer* between Montreal, New York, and Washington; the *Ambassador* and *New Englander* between Montreal, Springfield (Massachusetts), and Boston; the *Ocean Limited* and *Maritime Express* between Montreal and Halifax; the *Toronto* between Toronto and New York City; the *Gull* between Halifax and Boston; the *Owl* between Regina and Saskatoon; and the *Ontario Limited* between London and Toronto. These were in addition to secondary and branchline

CN

System Timetable
April 25, 1976-
October 30, 1976

Indicateur général
25 avril 1976-
30 octobre 1976

VIA—
Heralding the birth of a new era at CN. New name, new colours. Lively. Dynamic. Now on Turbo, VIA will progressively appear on all CN passenger trains.

VIA . . .
signe de la naissance d'un temps nouveau au CN. Nouveau nom, nouvelles couleurs vives, dynamiques, à la nouvelle image du CN. Déjà sur le Turbo, VIA apparaîtra progressivement sur tous les trains du CN.

Canadian National   Canadien National

In 1976 CN debuted the new VIA image on the *Turbo* train, as shown on the cover of this timetable. *Author collection*

The *Turbo* was not the only modernistic rail equipment to get a tryout on CN. The LRC (for lightweight, rapid, comfortable)—produced by a joint venture of Montreal Locomotive Works, Alcan, and Dofasco—was also introduced in the 1970s with somewhat more success than the *Turbo.* An LRC trainset is moved by a CN switcher at Montreal's Central Station in October 1982, while a boxcab electric waits to take a commuter train north through the Mount Royal Tunnel. *Steve Patterson*

trains—in all, enough to fill an 84-page timetable.

CN's passenger equipment was worn out by the end of World War II, but it was not until Donald Gordon started to renew the company's freight car fleet and dieselize its locomotive roster that he turned his attention to the passenger business. In 1953 CN ordered $59 million worth of lightweight, streamlined passenger cars: 218 coaches from Canadian Car & Foundry, and 141 sleeping, dining, and parlor cars from Pullman-Standard—enough to re-equip all the name trains on CN's major passenger routes. Arthur Dubin, in his book *More Classic Trains,* writes "every effort was made to distribute the rolling stock in such a manner that all Canadians benefited from the new trains."

CN promoted the purchase in advertising that described it as the dawn of "a new era in Canadian rail travel." In April 1955 a new transcontinental train, the *Super Continental,* was launched using the lightweight cars, and this equipment was the backbone of CN's passenger fleet for the next two decades. Yet it didn't have the glamour of CP's stainless steel transcontinental, the *Canadian,* which also premiered in 1955. CP's *Canadian* used 173 Budd-built cars, including domes, which CN was prevented from using because of the overhead wires at Central Station, Montreal. But the *Super Continental* was a major step forward for CN's passengers.

The next big change in the marketing and operation of CN's passenger service began in 1963. The essence of the new approach, as described by Donald MacKay, was "better service, cheaper fares and better equipment." It began with running passenger trains as a service, with dedicated management, rather than as an adjunct to everything else the railway did. Employees were trained to deal with passengers in a way that would make the customer want to come back to CN.

Initially, to test whether passengers could be lured back to the rails, CN tinkered with the *Ocean Limited*. An innovative pricing system was set up to achieve maximum revenue on the days where demand was normally greatest and to boost patronage on days when there were normally fewer riders. It was dubbed the "red, white and blue" fare structure. In July, for example, weekends were blue (high fare) and weekdays were white (medium fare); in February, weekends were white (medium fare) and weekdays were red (low fare). The result: a 50 percent increase in passengers.

The new approach was implemented across the railway. There were other changes, too, including the purchase of streamlined equipment from the Reading Company for use on a new Montreal–Quebec train, *Le Champlain*; use of former Milwaukee Road cars, both east and west (observation cars for Maritimes service and full-length domes in the Rockies); and the *Rapido* service between Montreal and Toronto, aimed at regaining business travelers who put a premium on time and convenience.

One experiment did not pan out. The Turbo train, built by United Aircraft, was a complete departure from traditional railroad engineering. It looked more like an aircraft than a train, and was powered by gas turbine engines. CN leased five sets of the equipment and put them into service between Montreal and Toronto in 1968, on a four-hour schedule. Their inaugural run for the press was marred by a collision with a truck at a road crossing near Kingston, Ontario, which left the nose of the lead power unit badly damaged and illustrated the equipment's vulnerability. The Turbos were also fuel-hungry machines, which made them uneconomical in an era of rising oil prices. Furthermore, their reliability was not good, and they were in and out of service throughout their careers, which lasted until the early 1980s.

Despite the success of CN's passenger-service initiatives of the 1960s, the company continued to lose money on passenger operations. In 1976 CN put both a new blue-and-yellow image on its passenger trains (starting with the Turbo) and a new name: VIA. CN hoped that turning the passenger operation into a separate operating unit would help dramatize the extent of its financial losses. VIA quickly evolved into a coordinated marketing effort by CN and CP, and by the fall of 1976 a "VIA" timetable had been issued that contained the passenger train schedules of both companies. Two years later, VIA Rail Canada became a crown corporation, following the business model used by Amtrak in the United States. The government would be financially responsible for rail passenger services and would contract with CN and CP for track access and other services.

CN management was happy to be rid of the financial losses associated with passenger services, but more than five decades of CN passenger trains had left their imprint on the Canadian consciousness.

One of the changes resulting from the operation of passenger trains by VIA Rail Canada was that electrically heated, rebuilt stainless steel cars from Canadian Pacific's *Canadian* started to appear on CN routes. VIA train 5. The *Skeena* from Jasper, Alberta, to Prince Rupert, British Columbia, is seen on CN's Skeena Subdivision in April 1992. This was the first operation of the former CP equipment on this train. *Phil Mason*

The Carbonear mixed train (*sans* freight cars) passes through Spaniards Bay, Newfoundland, in July 1984.
Steve Patterson

CHAPTER FIVE

FROM SEA TO SEA:
The Regions of CN

Fifty years ago Canadian National extended from St. John's, Newfoundland, in the east, to Churchill, Manitoba, in the north, and Vancouver Island, British Columbia, in the west. Today's CN does not reach any of those locations, but it still extends from the Atlantic to the Pacific and from the Gulf of Alaska (via a railcar barge service between Prince Rupert, British Columbia, and Whittier, Alaska) to the Gulf of Mexico (thanks to the acquisition of Illinois Central in 1999).

CN system map, 1971: Newfoundland, Maritime Provinces, Eastern Quebec, and Grand Trunk and Central Vermont lines in New England.
Author collection

Operations and traffic patterns have changed, but CN has remained a geographically diverse company as its network has changed to meet the needs of the North American economy. The Latin motto on Canada's coat of arms reads *A Mari Usque Ad Mare*, or "From Sea to Sea." It describes not only Canada but CN as well.

The Maritimes: Railroading at the Water's Edge

CN's lines in the maritime provinces of Nova Scotia and New Brunswick were inherited mainly from the Intercolonial Railway, whose

mainline ran from Halifax north to Truro, Nova Scotia, then northwest through Moncton, New Brunswick, to Matapédia, Quebec. From Matapédia, the line turned west and then southwest to run along the St. Lawrence River toward Rivière-du-Loup, Lévis (across the river from Quebec City), and Montreal.

The Intercolonial also had a line from Truro to Sydney, on Cape Breton Island. Rail access to Cape Breton was originally by ferry, but in 1954 the Canso Causeway was completed, allowing uninterrupted rail movements to and from the island. Other

In 1982 *M. V. Abegweit* replaced an older vessel of the same name on the run between Borden, Prince Edward Island, and Cape Tormentine, New Brunswick. The new "Abby" was more than 400 feet (121 meters) in length and was specially designed for handling railcars, as well as motor vehicles and passengers. Here the ship leaves Borden for the mainland in August 1984. *Steve Patterson*

A CN freight with two MLW RS3 units, led by CN 3021, crosses the Canso Causeway en route from Truro to Sydney, Nova Scotia, in September 1960. *Jim Shaughnessy*

INKORA

Train 41 from Charlottetown, Prince Edward Island, to the ferry at Borden stops at Kinkora at 9:16 a.m. on August 17, 1962, behind 1,200-horsepower FM-designed, CLC-built diesel No. 1639. *Jim Shaughnessy*

Intercolonial lines ran from Moncton to Saint John, New Brunswick, and from Chatham Junction to Fredericton, New Brunswick. The Intercolonial also operated the Prince Edward Island Railway.

The Intercolonial was not the only CN predecessor to serve the Maritimes. The Halifax & South Western Railway, controlled by Canadian Northern, ran from Halifax to Yarmouth, Nova Scotia, with a branch from Bridgewater to Port Wade, on the Bay of Fundy. CNoR also had a 60-mile (97-kilometer) coal line on Cape Breton,

Nova Scotia, which ran from Point Tupper to Inverness. The National Transcontinental Railway contributed one Maritime route to CN, from Moncton to Quebec City via Edmundston, New Brunswick. This line was shorter and ran closer to the border between Canada and Maine than did the Intercolonial's Moncton–Quebec City route.

The economic rationale for most of the rail lines in the maritime provinces had more to do with promoting local development than with generating a return on investment for the lines' various operators and owners. There was freight

to be sure. Both imports and exports moved via rail between Halifax and the rest of Canada. Saint John was also a major port city, although CN's circuitous route put it at a disadvantage versus Canadian Pacific, whose line between Saint John and Montreal ran east-west across Maine. In the area of Sydney, Nova Scotia both coal-mining and steel-making were sources of freight revenue. New Brunswick generated forest products—paper, pulpwood, and lumber—all of which moved by rail.

The conflict between the railways' need for better returns on their Maritime traffic and the protests of shippers who felt that they were at a disadvantage because rates, in their view, were too high, led to the passage of the Maritime Freight Rate Act in 1927. The act authorized the federal government to pay the railways a 20 percent subsidy on traffic that originated or terminated in the Maritimes.

For many years CN's lines in the Maritimes were best known for the vacation spots they reached. A 1937 CN travel brochure described the region's "smooth, sand-covered beaches over which rolls the surf from the Atlantic; inland vistas of smiling farms,

CN 1775 west at Martins River, Nova Scotia, in July 1984. This scene is 66 miles (106 kilometers) southwest of Halifax on the now-abandoned line to Yarmouth. *Steve Patterson*

CN 1753 west passes a potato warehouse at Albany, Prince Edward Island, in August 1984. *Steve Patterson*

meadows and gently rolling hills, forests and rivers; along the sea coast, picturesque fishing villages and deep-sea fisherman types."

To meet the need of vacationers, CN provided not only passenger trains (most notably the *Ocean Limited* and *Maritime Express* between Montreal and Halifax, both of which carried cars for Sydney), but also two hotels and a resort: the Nova Scotian Hotel in Halifax; the Charlottetown Hotel (originally the Canadian National Hotel) in Charlottetown, Prince Edward Island; and the Pictou Lodge, at Pictou, Nova Scotia.

Tourism remained an important element in the economy of the Maritimes over the decades, but vacationers do not generate freight business. As CN became more profit-oriented, many of its lines in the region were abandoned or, in two cases, turned over to independent operators. Rail operations on Prince Edward Island ended in 1989. The Halifax & South Western line to Yarmouth was abandoned in stages, with the last seg-

ment seeing service in 1993. By 2003, the former Intercolonial routes between Moncton and Campbellton, New Brunswick, and from Truro to Sydney, Nova Scotia, had both been turned over to regional rail operators.

Today, what remains of CN in the Maritimes is the Halifax–Moncton–Edmundston route, which serves as a major corridor for intermodal traffic moving between Halifax and inland points in Canada and the United States, as well as the line between Moncton and Saint John.

The Newfoundland Railway
The final component of CN's system in the Maritimes was the Newfoundland Railway. Newfoundland became Canada's tenth province on April 1, 1949, after more than three centuries as a British colony. One of the conditions of the agreement between Newfoundland and Canada was that the Canadian government would take over the island's railway.

Known as the "mini ore" train, CN train No. 587 operated from Campbellton, New Brunswick, to Brunswick Mines and back. The ore handled from the mine was dropped at the smelter at Belledune, and its weight required two six-axle Century-type locomotives. CN 2021 and 2014, delivered by Montreal Locomotive Works in 1968, are part of a group of 44 C630M units rostered by CN. The train is shown at Dalhousie Junction, New Brunswick, in February 1992 *George Pitarys*

Beginning in 1952 General Motors Diesel Division produced a unique series of locomotives, the six-axle (C-C) NF110 and NF210 models, for Newfoundland service. In this photo they show their family resemblance to the GP and SD models of the same era. This narrow-gauge freight train, en route from Port aux Basques to St. John's, is at Glenwood, Newfoundland, in May 1975. *Phil Mason*

Railway construction in Newfoundland began in 1881 with the building of a line west from the capital, St. John's. By 1884, an 86-mile (138-kilometer) line had been completed to Harbour Grace. To keep construction costs down, it was built to a gauge of 3 feet, 6 inches. Unlike other narrow gauge lines that were later converted to standard gauge, the Newfoundland Railway remained narrow gauge until the end.

In 1890 contractor Robert Gillespie Reid agreed to build an extension of the railway to the west, and in 1893 he signed a contract to operate the railway in return for land grants (5,000 acres per mile of railway). By 1898 a line had been completed to Port aux Basques at the western end of the island, a distance of 547 rail miles (881 kilometers). The Reid

Newfoundland Company became the operator of the railway for the next quarter-century and was also put in charge of Newfoundland's streetcar, telegraph, coastal ferry, and hydro-electric services.

Like other railway builders, Reid saw the railway as a development tool, but the economic pressures caused by World War I, and the downturn that followed the war, left the Reid Newfoundland Company unable to finance needed improvements. The company's contract was terminated in 1923, by which time the construction of various branchlines had given the island more than 900 miles (1,450 kilometers) of railway.

World War II found Newfoundland in a strategically advantageous location. Military bases were built at Argentia, Gander,

Stephenville, and St. John's, and the railway benefited from a doubling of freight traffic. But the end of the war brought a quick end to the traffic surge, and in 1949, when Newfoundlanders voted to join Canada, the federal government agreed to take over the money-losing island railway. CN found itself running not only the rail freight and passenger services, but also the island's telephone service, its ferry services, and the Hotel Newfoundland in St. John's, which CN thoroughly renovated to bring up to the standards of other CN hotels.

Management by CN brought many changes to the railway (which by this time was operating 705 route miles [1,135 kilometers] after several branchline abandonments). Wage levels for the railway's 4,100 employees

were increased, and CN invested in rail, cars, and diesel locomotives.

Newfoundland's economy benefited from confederation with Canada, and more freight started to move over the railway. However, the system for handling freight between CN's railhead at North Sydney, Nova Scotia, and the Newfoundland terminal at Port aux Basques was labor-intensive and time-consuming. Freight moving in either direction was unloaded from railcars, transferred to vessels piece by piece, ferried across the Cabot Strait, and then reloaded onto railcars.

As CN modernized the island's ferry service, a major improvement was the ability to carry standard gauge freight cars across the Cabot Strait. In the shop at Port aux Basques, standard gauge trucks were replaced

Aside from the NF110 and NF210 models, CN also bought from GMD an export-type locomotive, model G8, for Newfoundland service. These A1A-A1A units were lighter by about 50,000 pounds than their C-C cousins. Nos. 800 and 802 are at St. John's in July 1984, with the headquarters building of the Newfoundland rail system in the background. *Steve Patterson*

95

Despite the gauge difference, cars from CN's regular fleet could carry freight to Newfoundland destinations, as long as they had their wheels changed at Port aux Basques, as seen here in August 1984. Trucks were marked with car numbers so that a car would return to North Sydney, Nova Scotia, with its original equipment. *Steve Patterson*

In 1979 CN gave the Newfoundland freight service a new name, TerraTransport, and began a program of putting freight into containers so that it could reach customers without being transloaded between railcars and trucks. Once the traffic was in containers, it could be moved by truck anywhere on the island where there was a road. Rail transport became a costly luxury, and by 1984 all branchlines had been abandoned. Still, financial losses on the Newfoundland rail service persisted despite better equipment, improved operations, and cutbacks in the route map. The last train on the island ran in 1988.

Ontario and Quebec: Factories South, Forests North

The residents of Ontario and Quebec together represent more than 60 percent of Canada's population. They are the most diverse of the Canadian provinces, and CN's operations reflect this. They contain the highest-density segment in the CN network (Toronto–Montreal), as well as some of the lowest-density routes (the lines in northern Quebec). Two of the four major classification yards on the system are located here: Taschereau Yard in Montreal and MacMillan Yard in Toronto.

In southern Ontario and the urban areas of Quebec, smokestack industries—auto plants, steel mills, refineries, and chemical plants—predominate, whereas in the north, most rail traffic is either extracted from below ground or harvested from the coniferous forests that blanket the Canadian Shield. Overlaying the traffic that originates or terminates in these provinces is business (primarily intermodal) moving between Halifax in the east and customers in western Canada and the United States.

The three major contributors to what would become CN's network in these provinces were the Grand Trunk, Canadian Northern, and National Transcontinental railways. In addition, the Intercolonial route from Halifax entered Quebec at Matapédia, extending first to Rivière-du-Loup and

with narrow gauge. After the car went to its Newfoundland destination, it would return to Port aux Basques, the original trucks would be put back under the car, and it would make the ferry passage back to North Sydney. The narrow gauge could only handle cars of up to 50 tons (at a time when 100-ton cars were becoming a regular sight on many North American rail lines) but it was a big improvement over transloading. In addition to the service across the strait, CN also operated a number of coastal ferry services—a 1961 CN timetable shows nine vessels operating on 12 Newfoundland and Labrador coastal routes.

Newfoundland was not immune to changes in transportation that were occurring throughout North America. The Trans-Canada highway was completed across the island in 1965. *The Caribou* between St. John's and Port aux Basques (unofficially, the *Newfie Bullet*), which made 20 station stops plus 19 flag stops en route and averaged 24 miles per hour (39 kilometers per hour), was replaced by a bus in 1969. Mixed trains on the Argentia, Bonavista, and Carbonear branches survived into the 1970s.

Great Western Railway engine No. 42 ("Diadem") exits the Suspension Bridge at Niagara Falls, Ontario, in 1864. *National Archives of Canada/ PA-138681*

CN system map, 1971: Ontario, Quebec, Grand Trunk Western, and Duluth, Winnipeg & Pacific. *Author collection*

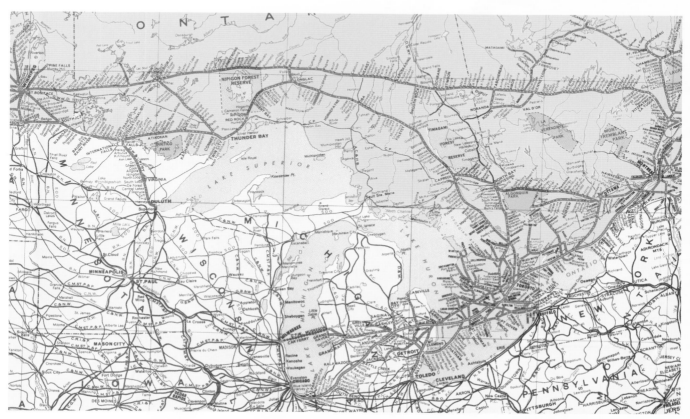

Train No. 416 emerges from miles of running through the northern Quebec wilderness as it passes Hervey Junction in August 1999. Originating in Arvida, the train is laden with finished aluminum blocks from the large Alcan plants in the Lac St. Jean region, as well as a heavy dose of wood and lumber products. *George Pitarys*

In 1929 CN rebuilt the former Grand Trunk shops at Point St. Charles, Montreal. The shop complex, shown here in 1930, covered 30 acres and employed approximately 2,500 people. *National Archives of Canada/ PA-037501*

The St. Lawrence River is never far away in southern Quebec and Ontario. Here CN 6767 pauses at Lévis, Quebec, with the westbound *Scotian* in June 1979. Across the river in Quebec City is Canadian Pacific's landmark hotel, the Chateau Frontenac. *Tom Murray*

The Quebec City-bound *Champlain,* using former Reading *Crusader* equipment, approaches the south end of the Quebec Bridge spanning the St. Lawrence River in August 1964. *Jim Shaughnessy*

Long since rendered obsolete by the discontinuance of passenger service and the installation of CTC signaling that sounded the death knell for train order operation, the well-preserved station at Rivière Bleu, Quebec, is witness to the passage of hot Halifax-to-Toronto intermodal train No. 149 in April 2001. *George Pitarys*

eventually to Lévis and Montreal. On Quebec's Gaspé Peninsula, CN acquired the Atlantic, Quebec & Western Railway and Quebec Oriental Railway in 1929.

The most heavily used lines in southern Quebec and Ontario are of GTR heritage, including the Quebec City–Montreal line, the double-track Montreal–Toronto line, and the route from Toronto to Hamilton, London, Sarnia, and Windsor, Ontario. CN also uses former GTR trackage (originally built by the Great Western Railway) to reach the Niagara gateway and Buffalo, New York.

As railways evolved, crossing the St. Lawrence and other major rivers was a significant engineering challenge. Notable milestones in the crossing of the region's waterways include:

• The Niagara River Suspension Bridge, opened by the Great Western Railway in 1855, which GTR replaced with a steel arch bridge in 1897.

• The Victoria Bridge over the St. Lawrence River at Montreal, opened by GTR in 1859 and rebuilt in place as a double-track steel truss structure in 1897 and 1898.

• The Quebec Bridge, a critical link in the National Transcontinental's mainline, and the world's largest railway cantilever bridge. As construction proceeded in 1907, one section of the bridge collapsed into the river, killing 73 workers. It was redesigned by a new team of engineers, but during the final phase of construction in 1916, the center span collapsed, claiming 13 lives. The bridge was completed in 1917.

From Toronto north, a former Canadian Northern route carries transcontinental traffic toward Winnipeg via Sudbury and Capreol. This was once part of CNoR's route from Toronto to Winnipeg by way of Port Arthur and Fort William, but CN's east-west route uses the Long Lake cutoff between Longlac and Nakina, and the former National Transcontinental line west of Nakina.

Between Winnipeg and Thunder Bay on the former CNoR route, there are two main traffic flows: grain, coal, potash, and other commodities moving to Thunder Bay; and western Canadian resources en route to U.S. markets via the Duluth, Winnipeg & Pacific Railway, which leaves the CNoR route at Fort Frances, Ontario. The ex-CNoR line between Thunder Bay and Longlac carries relatively little traffic today.

North of Montreal and Quebec City, the former National Transcontinental line and various CN-built branchlines carry forest products and minerals. However, the

CN's defining physical characteristic in much of southern Quebec and Ontario is its proximity to the St. Lawrence River, the Great Lakes, and their connecting waterways. The region's first railways were designed to connect rivers rather than to compete with them, and CN still depends on port facilities along the St. Lawrence, particularly at Montreal, for substantial volumes of traffic.

CN train No. 364 south of Blackburn, Quebec, on May 16, 2003, is not far from Chambord, the hub of rail activity in the Lac St. Jean region. The woods the train traverses represent an important portion of the business on this piece of the railway. *George Pitarys*

National Transcontinental line is no longer transcontinental, having been abandoned between La Sarre, Quebec, and Cochrane, Ontario, and between Calstock and Nakina, Ontario. The segment between Cochrane and Calstock is now operated by Ontario Northland Railway.

Several former CN lines in Ontario and Quebec have been taken over by short-line and regional rail operators over the past two decades. In Quebec, they include lines from Matapédia to Pabos; Pabos to Gaspé; Limilou to Clermont; Norton, Vermont, to Ste. Rosalie, Quebec; and Mont-Joli, Quebec, to Campbellton, New Brunswick. In Ontario independent operators connecting with CN now provide service from St. Thomas to Delhi; Port Colborne to St. Catharines; Glen Robertson to Hawksbury; Stratford Junction to Goderich; Brantford to Nanticoke; and Pembroke, Ontario, to Coteau, Quebec.

A number of unprofitable and redundant CN lines in the region have been abandoned. However, given the rail-oriented nature of many industries in Ontario and Quebec, and

the critical geographic position these two provinces occupy in terms of North American freight flows, it is safe to say that they will retain their prominent position in the CN route map.

The Prairies: Land of Wheat and Barley

Think of the provinces of Manitoba, Saskatchewan, and Alberta, and the image that comes to mind is a grain elevator against an expanse of broad sky and flat landscape. That image is accurate, but far from complete. In many places, the prairies are not so much flat as they are rolling, with north-south watercourses that railway builders had to contend with as they built from east to west. In addition, all three of these provinces stretch far to the north into mineral-rich areas, some of which took many years for the rail system to penetrate. Besides grain and minerals (notably nickel and copper), the prairie provinces are the source of substantial potash production (in southern Saskatchewan) and petroleum products (in Alberta). Alberta is also home to the eastern slopes of the Canadian Rockies and their large coal deposits.

Two of CN's predecessor lines were responsible for most of the trackage that CN inherited in these provinces: Canadian Northern, which got its start in Manitoba, and eventually reached west toward Vancouver, and Grand Trunk Pacific, which built its own route from Winnipeg to Prince Rupert, British Columbia. The National Transcontinental also reached Winnipeg, but only 75 miles (121 kilometers) of its route was within Manitoba.

In its timetables Canadian Northern called itself the "Saskatchewan Valley Route:

The Homeseekers' Way to Western Canada Through Winnipeg." Its lines criss-crossed the prairies, with three principal east-west routes and a variety of other lines serving the region. The CNoR mainline ran from Winnipeg west through Portage la Prairie, Gladstone, and Dauphin, Manitoba; Canora, Warman, and North Battleford, Saskatchewan; and Lloydminster, Edmonton, and Jasper, Alberta. Just west of Jasper, the line entered British Columbia. A secondary CNoR route took a more southerly route, passing through Brandon, Manitoba, and Regina, Saskatchewan, before reaching Saskatoon, while a connecting line reached

CN system map, 1971: Prairie Provinces. *Author collection*

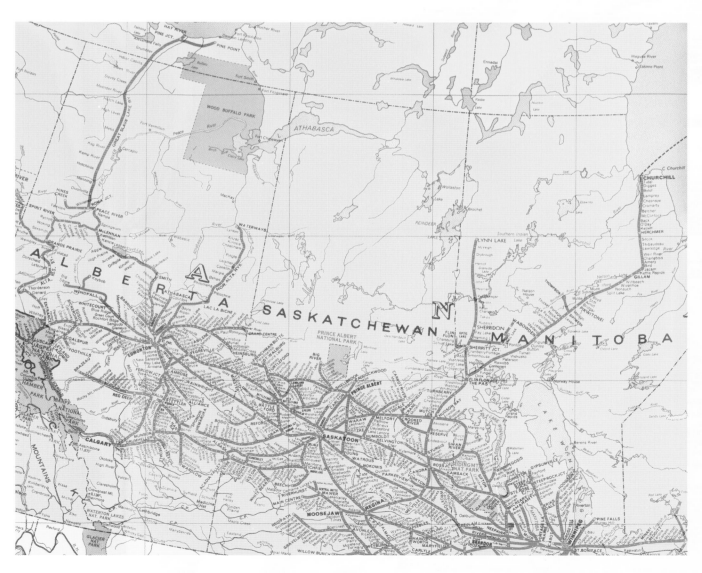

The rolling nature of the terrain in parts of the prairie provinces can create opportunities for snow to accumulate in cuts, particularly those with steep slopes. According to the notes that accompanied this 1947 photo in the CN archives, CN No. 2814 and two other steam engines and plow were being dug out of a drift near Victoria Plains, Saskatchewan, "as work continued to open blockade. Took five days to open drift. Drift was almost a mile long and completely covered pole line in places." *Canada Science and Technology Museum, CSTM/CN collection neg. no. X24091*

west from Saskatoon to Drumheller and Calgary, Alberta. A more northerly east-west route branched off the mainline near Dauphin, Manitoba, and served Melfort and Prince Albert, Saskatchewan, before rejoining the mainline at North Battleford.

As a latecomer, following both the Canadian Pacific and CNoR across the prairies, GTP had a less extensive network than its rivals. Its mainline west of Winnipeg was north of the CP and south of the CNoR. It passed through Portage la Prairie and Rivers, Manitoba, (with a short branch south to Brandon); Melville, Saskatoon, and Biggar, Saskatchewan; and Wainwright, Edmonton, Edson, and Jasper, Alberta, before entering British Columbia to continue toward Prince

Rupert. The GTP line is now CN's mainline across the region. In its short life GTP did construct some prairie branchlines, including Melville to Regina, Saskatchewan; Regina to a connection with the Great Northern Railway at Northgate, Alberta; Regina to Moose Jaw and Riverhurst, Saskatchewan; Melville to Canora, Saskatchewan; Watrous to Prince Albert, Saskatchewan; Biggar to Loverna, Saskatchewan; and the Alberta Coal Branch, running south from Edson.

Together with fertilizers, grain accounts for more than 20 percent of CN's revenues in a good crop year. Wheat is the grain most often associated with the Canadian prairies, but they are a source of barley, oats, rye, flax, and other crops as well. In the past 30 years

A set of three GMD1 units led by CN 1032 are seen at Kindersley, Saskatchewan, on a ballast train in June 1976. *Stan Smaill*

CN GP38-2 7528 works as part of a hump set shoving cars over the crest and into the classification tracks at Symington Yard in Winnipeg in October 1992. A Beltpack console is remotely controlling the locomotive. CN was the first major railway to use this technology, which has since been implemented by other rail carriers in yards and terminals throughout North America. *Phil Mason*

CN SD40 5233 and a GP9 pass the Pioneer elevator at Biggar, Saskatchewan, in May 1976 with an eastbound train carrying forest products. Biggar, population 2,351, is a crew change point between Saskatoon and Edmonton. A sign on the outskirts of town reads, "New York is Big But This is Biggar." *Phil Mason*

the system of gathering and transporting grain on the prairies has been modernized. One of the biggest changes has been the conversion from railway-supplied boxcars with grain doors (which would often leak grain on the ground) to 100-ton covered hopper cars financed by the government. There are fewer elevators today than 30 years ago, with more grain now moving through large facilities where unit trains can be loaded. In 2003 CN reported that it had 75 high-throughput elevators located on its lines, capable of loading 50- to 100-car trains.

Some of the lowest-density grain branch-lines, where GMD1 locomotives once tiptoed along light rail, are now gone, and others have been taken over by short-line and regional railroads. In fact, while Canada was late in arriving at a system for transferring low-density lines from large railroads to independent short-line operators, the first significant step in that direction came in the prairies with the creation of Alberta's Central Western Railway in 1986. Aside from the Central Western, which operates a former CN line north of Dinosaur Junction, Alberta, several other prairie lines, now controlled by independent operators, gather grain traffic and interchange it to CN for the line haul. In Manitoba, these include lines from Winnipeg to Pine Falls; Winnipeg to Carman; and Morris to Elgin; and in Saskatchewan, the routes from Saskatoon to Prince Albert, from Denholm to Meadow Lake, and from Moose Jaw to Parry.

Although there is some truck transportation of grain on the prairies, for these crops to reach export and most domestic markets, rail transportation is the only practical way to go. Because of its route structure, CN will continue to be a key player in the grain transportation system regardless of how that system may change in the future.

Reaching Northward

Beginning in 1912 three privately built railways extended rail service into the sparsely populated country north and northwest of Edmonton. By 1920 the government of Alberta had leased two of the lines and contracted out their operation to Canadian Pacific; the government operated the third line. In 1926 the government terminated the CP contract, and CN began operating the lines, which by then included a fourth route built by the government.

Examples of cooperation between CP and CN in the 1920s were rare, but the two companies did join forces in 1929 to operate these lines under the banner of Northern Alberta Railways (NAR). The joint arrangement lasted until 1981, when CP bowed out and the NAR routes became part of CN.

From Edmonton one NAR line ran northeast to Lac La Biche and Fort McMurray. Most of the railway's mileage was northwest of Edmonton, however. NAR ran through Slave Lake to McClennan, where one line continued

There is no question about what drives the local economy at Rosebud, Alberta, as CN 9169 rolls through in June 1983 on train No. 316. Rosebud is 60 miles (97 kilometers) northeast of Calgary, on the former Canadian Northern line to Saskatoon. When this photo was taken, the line had 85-pound rail, and motive power on through freights was typically a mix of F7 and GP9 units. The line was subsequently rebuilt to handle heavier locomotives. *Phil Mason*

During construction of the Great Slave Lake Railway between 1966 and 1969, an automatic train operation system developed by Westinghouse was installed in four GP9 locomotives. The system provided automatic speed control on the mainline, and a remote-control system for switching. The latter was a precursor to the Beltpack system developed in the 1980s by the CN Technical Research Centre (now part of CN's consulting affiliate, CANAC). Here, a GSL employee uses the remote-control system in 1968. *Canada Science and Technology Museum, CSTM/CN collection neg. no. 68533–20*

northwest to Peace River and Hines Creek, while another ran west to Spirit River, then south to Grande Prairie, before turning northwest toward Dawson Creek, British Columbia. NAR's total mileage was approximately 920 miles (1,481 kilometers).

Much of NAR's traffic consisted of grain. However, when the Great Slave Lake Railroad (GSL, a CN-operated line that connected with NAR at Roma Junction, just west of Peace River) opened in 1968, lead and zinc ore taken from a Cominco zinc- and copper-mining operation at Pine Point, Alberta, and destined for the Cominco smelter at Trail in southern British Columbia, began to move over the line.

The 430-mile (692-kilometer) GSL was built and operated by CN for the federal government. It was the first and only rail line to extend into Canada's Northwest Territories. CN historian Donald MacKay observes that the GSL (and NAR) "hauled out grain and lumber and became the main supply line for Arctic oil exploration. By linking the Northern Alberta Railways to Hay River, the staging point for the Mackenzie River barge system, CN lowered the cost of shipments not only to Yellowknife but the Mackenzie delta and the Arctic coast."

The 230-mile (370-kilometer) Alberta Resources Railway (ARR), financed by the province of Alberta and operated by CN, opened in 1969 from Swan Landing (on the mainline between Jasper and Hinton) to Grande Cache and Grande Prairie, where it connected with NAR. This line was built to serve a coal mine in the Smoky River region and to open up markets for grain and lumber producers in northern Alberta.

Today, independent short-line and regional carriers operate most of the former NAR and the entire GSL and ARR lines.

Another line that pushed toward Canada's sub-Arctic was the Hudson Bay line. According to G. R. Stevens, the idea of such a line was first proposed in 1885 in response to grain producers' desire to have an alternative to the CP monopoly on the prairies. In

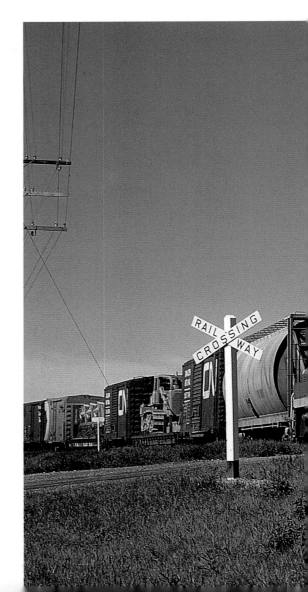

1905 William Mackenzie and Donald Mann of the CNoR got involved and mapped out a 538-mile (866-kilometer) route from Prairie River, Saskatchewan, to Port Nelson, Manitoba. In 1924 the terminus was changed to Churchill, Manitoba, and a new route was surveyed, but it was not until 1931 that the line finally opened.

Despite the theoretical appeal of the Hudson Bay route for grain destined to Europe, the reality is that the Port of Churchill is closed roughly eight months out of the year. Less than 3 percent of Canada's grain exports move through the port annually. Nevertheless, the line gained notoriety during its years under CN as the "polar bear route," due to the bears that are a common sight around Churchill. But the line was a drain on CN from the time it was completed. In 1997 its operation was taken over by Denver-based short-line operator OmniTRAX, which operates it as the Hudson Bay Railway.

Other northern extensions included:
• A 144-mile (232-kilometer) line to Lynn Lake, Manitoba, completed in November 1953 and built to tap into the region's nickel, copper, and cobalt deposits.
• A 161-mile (259-kilometer) line from Beattyville to Chibougamau, Quebec (in another mineral rich-area), opened in 1957. This was followed by the construction of a 133-mile (214-kilometer) connecting line from Cache Lake to St. Felicien, Quebec, which opened in 1959.

Northern Alberta Railways Nos. 404-202 are at Carbondale, Alberta, 20 miles (32 kilometers) north of Edmonton, in June 1976. Following the merger of NAR into CN in 1981, this segment was abandoned in favor of the CN line between Dunvegan Yard, Edmonton, and Morinville, Alberta. *Phil Mason*

• A 52-mile (84-kilometer) line from Optic Lake to Chisel Lake, Manitoba, built to serve the Hudson Bay Mining and Smelting Company, which opened in 1960.

CN in the West: Toward the Pacific Rim

At its peak in the 1970s, CN's network west of Edmonton consisted of:

• The Grand Trunk Pacific line from Edmonton to Jasper, Alberta, and Red Pass Junction, British Columbia. (Most of CNoR's parallel line was removed during World War I to provide rail for the war effort.)

• The Alberta Coal Branch south of Edson, built by GTP.

• The Alberta Resources Railway north of Swan Landing.

• The CNoR route from Red Pass Junction to Vancouver via Blue River, Kamloops, and Boston Bar, British Columbia.

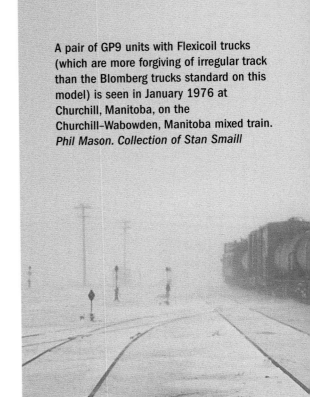

A pair of GP9 units with Flexicoil trucks (which are more forgiving of irregular track than the Blomberg trucks standard on this model) is seen in January 1976 at Churchill, Manitoba, on the Churchill–Wabowden, Manitoba mixed train. *Phil Mason. Collection of Stan Smaill*

CN No. 1147 is shown on VIA No. 291, the Lynn Lake mixed train, at The Pas, Manitoba, in October 1988. *Phil Mason*

Crews arriving on VIA train 93 at Churchill in October 1991 did not have to go far for their lodging—they stayed on the second floor of the depot. *Steve Patterson*

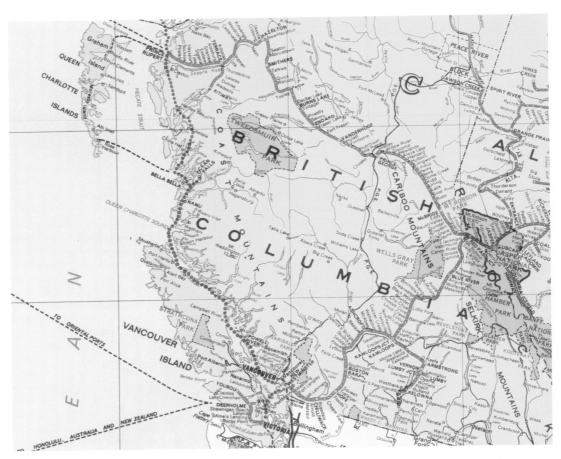

• The Okanagan route from Kamloops to Kelowna, British Columbia, completed by CN in 1925.
• CNoR lines on Vancouver Island.
• The GTP line from Red Pass Junction to Prince Rupert, British Columbia.
• The Kitimat Subdivision, south of Terrace, British Columbia, opened by CN in 1955 to serve a smelter run by the Aluminum Company of Canada.

Grand Trunk Pacific and Canadian Northern were latecomers to western Canada. CP had completed its transcontinental line in 1885. It chose a southern route over the Rockies via Kicking Horse Pass with grades as steep as 4.5 percent. CP subsequently rebuilt the line with a pair of spiral tunnels that reduced the ruling grade to 2.2 percent.

CP's choice of the southern route left a much easier grade via Yellowhead Pass available for both GTP and CNoR. GTP got there first, reaching the continental divide in November 1911. Its ruling grade was 0.5 percent westbound and 0.4 percent eastbound, except for a 19-mile (31-kilometer) segment approaching Yellowhead Pass, where the eastbound grade was 1.0 percent (later eased by CN's construction of a new connection between the former GTP and CNoR lines).

CNoR also used the Yellowhead crossing on its route to Vancouver, reaching the pass in 1913. G. R. Stevens describes this as "perhaps the most foolish trackage ever to be built in Canada." Since both GTP and CNoR received government assistance for their western extensions, "the taxpayer was therefore building two-lines across well-nigh trafficless territory within a stone's throw of each other," Stevens writes. However, the duplication did not last long; in 1916 work began on removing sections of the CNoR line so that

Soldiers of a construction battalion remove rail from the Canadian Northern line between Edmonton and Yellowhead Pass, circa 1917. The rail was shipped to Europe for use in constructing rail lines to support the military effort during World War I. *National Archives of Canada/ C-068790*

CN 5340 west at Henry House, Alberta, a few miles east of Jasper, in October 1989. *Steve Patterson*

In 1924 CN constructed a wharf at Cowichan Bay on Vancouver Island, where lumber from the island's forests could be transferred from railcar to vessel. *Canada Science and Technology Museum, CSTM/CN collection neg. no. 250*

the rail could be shipped to Europe for use in the war. The former CNoR grade, as well as remains of bridge foundations, can still be seen in some locations today.

From Kamloops west, CNoR found that being 30 years behind the CP put it at a disadvantage. Through the Thompson and Fraser River canyons, CP had chosen the easier side of the river for its route; CNoR, by default, took the more difficult side. Between Kamloops and Boston Bar, a distance of 125 miles (201 kilometers), the line crosses the Thompson River eight times and the Fraser twice, and originally had 17 tunnels.

Although Vancouver was CNoR's western objective, CP and Great Northern (GN) were already there. GN was willing to provide CNoR with access to Vancouver through the sale of one track segment and trackage rights over another segment. The western end of CNoR construction was at a location it designated Port Mann, about 15 miles (24 kilometers) east of Vancouver, where it built a yard and other servicing facilities.

Today the CN line to Vancouver carries grain, potash, sulfur, and other bulk commodities for export, as well as a large volume of international container traffic. Tunnels were enlarged in the early 1990s to accommodate double-stack equipment. Traffic density on the Vancouver–Edmonton line in 2002 was more than 50 million gross ton-miles, or only about 15 percent less than the volume carried by CN's Montreal–Toronto mainline. The latter, however, is double-track, reverse-signaled, high-capacity railway with long stretches of tangent track; the Vancouver line through the river canyons of British Columbia is single-track with many speed restrictions due to curves.

In 1999 CN and CP began a paired-track arrangement for 155 miles (249 kilometers) in the Thompson and Fraser canyon area. Both CN and CP trains now use CN's line westbound and CP's eastbound. The arrangement increases capacity by eliminating the delays inherent in having trains meet each other in single-track territory.

One price that CNoR paid for financial assistance from the British Columbia provincial government was a requirement to construct a

At Cisco, British Columbia, CN and Canadian Pacific exchange sides of the Fraser River. In this August 1981 photo, a westbound CN freight behind SD40 5154 crosses from the west side of the river to the east, while an eastbound CP freight simultaneously crosses the bridge in the foreground. *Steve Patterson*

rail line on Vancouver Island. Work began in 1911, but because of war-related delays the first segment was not opened until 1917. Canadian National completed the Vancouver Island lines in the 1920s, in the process penetrating some of the best logging territory in Canada. However, a typical CN haul for lumber moving to the ferry slip at Cowichan Bay was only 30 miles (48 kilometers), so the economics of this operation were never good. By 1991 CN had ceased operating on Vancouver Island.

Another piece of unfinished business left by CNoR was in the Okanagan territory of southern British Columbia. CNoR had planned a route for the line, but did not begin construction before being absorbed by CN. The 119-mile (192-kilometer) line from Kamloops to Kelowna, which used parts of two CP subdivisions to reach its southern terminus, was completed in 1925. It operates as an independent short line today.

The GTP line to Prince Rupert, commonly known on CN as the B. C. North line,

was built on the theory that Prince Rupert's relative proximity to Asia would give it an advantage over Vancouver in capturing trans-Pacific trade. Yet the rail route from Jasper to Vancouver is 529 miles (852 kilometers), versus 722 miles (1,162 kilometers) to Prince Rupert—a difference of 193 miles (311 kilometers). Other things being equal, freight will generally seek a route that minimizes land mileage even if the route increases in water mileage. And conditions have never been equal between the two ports—Vancouver was a well-established port city before the first train from the east ever reached Prince Rupert.

Following World War I Prince Rupert's freight business was in the doldrums, but it did enjoy a substantial volume of passenger traffic, both as a gateway to Alaska and as part of the Triangle Tour (Vancouver–Jasper–Prince Rupert) promoted heavily by CN's passenger department. World War II brought the port into a prominent role for its strategic location, and the CN line was upgraded to

handle the resulting volume of traffic. CN's original road diesel locomotive, No. 9000, was equipped with armor plate to power a train with four gun-equipped flatcars that protected the CN line between Prince Rupert and Terrace. Gun emplacements were also constructed along the track near Prince Rupert.

In the 1980s a new grain terminal was constructed on Ridley Island, south of the city of Prince Rupert, and today an average of

An eastbound train passes through the Cape Horn rock sheds, east of Lasha, British Columbia, in the White Canyon of the Thompson River Canyon, in April 1996. *Phil Mason*

Kitwanga, British Columbia, is located 154 miles (248 kilometers) east of Prince Rupert. In October 1978, CN 9173, a rebuilt F7, leads a westbound freight. *Stan Smaill*

five trains per week arrive there with export grain. Prince Rupert also enjoyed a healthy volume of export coal traffic from the Tumbler Ridge area of British Columbia (originated by BC Rail) from 1983 to 2003, when the mines closed. As of early 2004 the coal facilities at Ridley Island were being used for iron ore moving from Minnesota to China. The Aquatrain service, which moves freight on the world's largest railcar barge (with a capacity of 50 cars) to a connection with the Alaska Railroad at Whittier, Alaska, also puts traffic on the Prince Rupert line. The barge makes 32 trips per year.

East of Prince George, where CN interchanges with BC Rail (the former Pacific Great Eastern Railway), traffic volumes are somewhat higher. CN receives about 300 cars of lumber per week from BC Rail origins for movement eastward. That volume is likely to increase following CN's planned acquisition of the provincially owned BC Rail franchise in 2004. As part of the deal with British Columbia, CN has offered to improve clearances on the Prince Rupert line to allow for the movement of double-stack intermodal trains to a proposed container port. Given capacity constraints on the rail lines to Vancouver, it is possible that Prince Rupert may finally achieve the level of business hoped for by Grand Trunk president Charles Melville Hays, who envisioned this "port at the end of the rainbow."

CN mixed train No. 297 is in the siding at Aleza Lake, British Columbia (between McBride and Prince George), so that freight train 1st 720, with F7 CN 9132 leading, can roll by on the main. *Tom Murray*

VIA train No. 10, eastbound from Prince Rupert to Jasper, approaches Red Pass Junction (west of Jasper) in July 1981. *Steve Patterson*

CN 5414 and BC Rail 4616 lead a freight next to the Thompson River at Martel, British Columbia, in June 1991. *CN*

GTW No. 5802 is eastbound at Griffith, Indiana, 30 miles (48 kilometers) east of Chicago, and headed for Battle Creek, Michigan, in May 1973. It is about to cross two railroads: the Erie Lackawanna and the Elgin, Joliet & Eastern. *Tom Murray*

CHAPTER SIX

CN'S U.S. AFFILIATES

Canadian National has always been more than a Canadian company. One of its predecessors, Grand Trunk Railway, was easily the most international railway in North America. It served New England in the east, Quebec and Ontario in the center of its network, and the heartland states of Michigan, Indiana, and Illinois in the west. Another CN predecessor, Canadian Northern, reached as far south as Duluth, Minnesota.

In 1971 Grand Trunk Western, which had used CN colors on its diesels for more than 20 years, started to differentiate itself by using blue instead of black on an order of 12 GP38AC units, numbered 5800 through 5811. Several of these units were subsequently transferred to Central Vermont. In October 1993, CV No. 5807 and 5811 handle a cut of cars next to the Conrail Boston & Albany line at Palmer, Massachusetts. *Brian Solomon*

Over time, the functions and strategic importance of CN's U.S. routes have changed. CN eventually left New England, but its Midwestern U.S. lines have become critical links in the railway's evolving route structure.

Central Vermont Railway

The Central Vermont (CV) had its roots in two early Vermont railway ventures: Vermont Central, which began operations in 1848 between White River Junction and Bethel, and Vermont & Canada, which opened in 1850 from Essex Junction to St. Albans. Eventually the two railroads connected with each other and came under common control. In 1873 Central Vermont Railroad was incorporated as a holding company for both of these ventures.

The other important component of the Central Vermont was the New London Northern, a predecessor of which opened in 1848. The New London Northern ultimately ran north from its namesake city in Connecticut, through Massachusetts, to Brattleboro, Vermont. Between Brattleboro and Windsor, Vermont, the south end of the Vermont Central, there was a gap, which was filled by the Boston & Maine (B&M), whose Connecticut River route was intertwined with those of CV and its predecessors.

At various points in the nineteenth century, CV and its constituents controlled lines extending into southern Quebec and northern New York State, as well as the Rutland Railroad and a steamship line on Lake Ontario. Yet the railway never prospered, making its securities inexpensive and creating an opportunity for GTR. Given the shortcomings of its route to Portland, Maine, GTR management saw an opportunity to develop long-haul business by using CV's line to New London and coastal vessels beyond to reach the ports of New York City and Boston. By 1885 GTR had gained financial control over CV, and in 1898 the company was reincorporated as Central Vermont Railway under GTR management.

The idea of connecting directly to a major New England port persisted, and in 1912 work began on a new 75-mile (121-kilometer) line from the CV at Palmer, Massachusetts, to the port of Providence, Rhode Island. That year, however, GTR's president, Charles Melville Hays, the chief proponent of the new line, died in the sinking of the *Titanic,* and the Providence extension was never completed.

Following the creation of CN in June 1919, the new parent company's devotion to CV was tested by a disastrous flood in November 1927. The penalty that CV paid for following easy-grade, water-level routes for much of its distance was that rising flood waters wiped out 21 bridges and much of the railway's track structure. Thirty miles (48 kilometers) of CV's mainline were rebuilt at a cost of $3 million, and the line reopened for business in February 1928.

CV's heaviest passenger traffic was north of White River Junction, where trains were interchanged with the B&M. Through service commenced between Montreal and Washington, D.C., in 1924 (the *Washingtonian* and the

In May 1976 a passenger excursion on the Central Vermont crosses the northern end of Lake Champlain at East Alburg, Vermont. *Stan Smaill*

Central Vermont train No. 744 rolls southbound through Leverett, Massachusetts, in December 1978, with three GP9 units—one Grand Trunk and two CV. The two CV units, Nos. 4928 and 4923, are former passenger engines. *Tom Murray*

Montrealer), and between Montreal and Boston two years later (the *New Englander* and the *Ambassador*). The Montreal–Washington trains survived until the end of CV passenger service in 1966.

But CV's route structure never served it well as a freight hauler. In partnership with CN and Grand Trunk Western, it operated a pair of fast freights between Chicago and New London (train Nos. 490 and 491), but the essential problem was that CV didn't serve many locations of commercial importance. It depended on connections—mainly with B&M as well as the New Haven, which was absorbed by Penn Central in 1969—to

CV train No. 324 crosses the White River at West Hartford, Vermont, in October 1993. CN 9401 and 9405 are both from a group of 233 GP40-2L(W) units delivered in 1974 and 1975. GTW 6204, a GP38 built in 1966, was originally DT&I 204. *Brian Solomon*

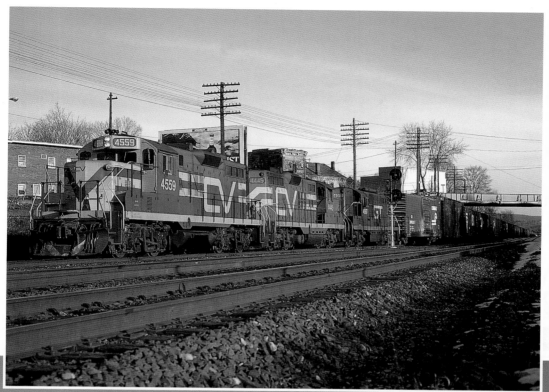

This CV motive power consist at Palmer, Massachusetts, in December 1987, documents the changing image of the railroad and the changing identities of individual locomotives. CV Nos. 4559 and 4445 were originally GT units. The trailing unit, No. 4917, is one of several engines transferred from GTW to CV. *Brian Solomon*

In the 1970s Grand Trunk locomotives were frequently found on Central Vermont, and vice versa. Here, GT 4906 and 4558 are northbound with CV train No. 511 at Randolph, Vermont. *Tom Murray*

originate or terminate freight. They had their own interests to protect and other connecting lines to choose from. As those carriers slid into bankruptcy (New Haven in 1961, B&M and Penn Central in 1970), they cut back on train service and maintenance budgets, making it harder than ever for CV to keep freight traffic on the rails.

Following the creation of Grand Trunk Corporation as a holding company for CN's U.S. subsidiaries in 1971, management tried to breathe life into CV by investing in distribution centers, where commodities like lumber and cement could be transferred from rail to truck. The company also trimmed operating expenses, put more of an emphasis on local management (such as by moving train

dispatchers from Montreal to St. Albans), and started an innovative intermodal service for lumber customers. It was not enough to make CV profitable.

After trying and failing to sell CV in 1982, CN management put it back on the market in the 1990s. By this time several companies had emerged that specialized in purchasing or leasing financially challenged lines from the major rail carriers. Using a combination of nontraditional labor arrangements, local management, and close attention to customer requirements, they were often able to turn a profit where a larger railway could not. One such company, RailTex, stepped forward to acquire CV, which was reborn as New England Central Railroad.

RailTex was subsequently acquired by RailAmerica, which continues to operate New England Central today.

Grand Trunk in New England

People did not use the term "globalization" in the 1840s, when the idea of a rail line between Montreal and Portland, Maine, was born. However, the builders of the Atlantic & St. Lawrence in the United States and its connecting line, the St. Lawrence & Atlantic in Quebec, were motivated by a similar idea: that international borders should not stand in the way of trade and commerce.

The specific commerce that the backers of these railways were after was grain and lumber traffic destined for Europe and other overseas destinations, much of which moved through the port of Montreal. The winter freezing of the St. Lawrence River made Montreal's port business seasonal, and John Alfred Poor saw an opportunity in this. Poor (the brother of Henry Varnum Poor, founder of what later became Standard & Poor's) led the effort by the city of Portland to secure a rail line to Montreal, in competition with Boston merchants who had similar ideas. The relatively short distance of the land-and-water route between Montreal and London via Portland won the day. The 300-mile (483-kilometer) railway through Maine, New Hampshire, Vermont, and Quebec was completed in 1853 and leased to Grand Trunk Railway of Canada the following year.

For a variety of reasons, the line never prospered to the degree that Poor had envisioned. Since water transport is inherently less expensive than rail, Montreal kept most

A northbound freight on the Grand Trunk, running from Island Pond, Vermont, to Sherbrooke, Quebec, crosses a trestle near Norton, Vermont, in June 1953. GT 2-8-2 Mikado No. 3703 was a 1918 product of Alco's Schenectady, New York, shop. *Jim Shaughnessy*

For more than 70 years this grain elevator was a landmark on the Portland, Maine, waterfront. Yet grain traffic peaked early in the twentieth century, and in 1971, when these three CN GP9 units were preparing to depart with GT train No. 393 for Montreal, the elevator had been unused for decades. It was dismantled a few years later. *Tom Murray*

of its port business during the warmer months. Following Confederation in 1867, and the building of the Intercolonial Railway, political considerations favored all-weather Canadian ports (Halifax and Saint John) over those in the United States.

Long after parent Grand Trunk Railway System had become part of Canadian National, the U.S. portion of the route (between Norton, Vermont, and Portland)

continued to be known as the Grand Trunk, and equipment was painted to reflect this well into the diesel era. To distinguish it from Grand Trunk Western, some tariffs referred to the line as "Grand Trunk (Eastern)," but it was not a separate corporation, nor did it have its own management, as did CN's other U.S. subsidiaries. When Grand Trunk Corporation was formed in 1971 as the parent company for CN's other

MAINE COAST
AND THE WHITE AND
GREEN MOUNTAINS

GRAND TRUNK
RAILWAY SYSTEM

CANADIAN NATIONAL
RAILWAYS

CN promoted tourism on the Grand Trunk through publications such as this one, produced in 1928. *Author collection*

U.S. subsidiaries, the route to Portland stayed under direct CN control.

The biggest single traffic generator was a large paper mill at Berlin, New Hampshire, but it was served by B&M as well as by GT. Other than forest products, the Montreal–Portland line had little local business. The line did enjoy a substantial passenger business during the summer, when residents of Quebec flocked to the beaches along the Maine coast, and New Englanders traveled north to resort towns like Poland Spring, Maine.

The vision of early Canadian railway builders like Francis Hincks, who in the

1850s had dreamed of a commercial route from Portland to Chicago through Canada, was borne out more than a century later when, in the 1970s, the GT route became an important link between Maine's paper producers and customers in the Midwest. Traffic managers at paper mills located on Maine Central could and did route many carloads to customers in the Midwestern United States via Yarmouth Junction and Danville Junction, where Maine Central interchanged the cars to GT. This overhead traffic had long been part of GT's

GT train No. 393 is operating as an extra train, and in accordance with CN operating rules of the time, carries white flags as it arrives at Berlin, New Hampshire, in June 1972. *Tom Murray*

revenue base, but in the 1970s GT and CN traffic volumes benefited from the financial and operational woes of the other outlet for westbound traffic from Maine, the B&M. GT train 393, the daily freight to Montreal, would typically leave Portland with only a handful of cars, but by the time it departed Danville Junction it might have 60 cars in tow.

Even with the overhead traffic, GT remained a light-density line. In the 1980s deregulation and other changes in the rail industry made it harder for John Poor's railroad to compete for business. In 1989 the line from Portland to Island Pond, Vermont, was sold to Emons Development Corporation. Emons later picked up a portion of the connecting line

The Largest Railway System in America

CANADIAN NATIONAL RAILWAYS
GRAND TRUNK RAILWAY SYSTEM • CENTRAL VERMONT RAILWAY
DULUTH, WINNIPEG AND PACIFIC RAILWAY

in Quebec. Today those routes are part of regional rail operator Genesee & Wyoming.

Grand Trunk Western Railroad

In the 1850s achieving access to Chicago was an important objective of Grand Trunk Railway's promoters and builders. It finally attained that goal in 1879, and Chicago traffic was soon generating more than 40 percent of GTR's revenues. GTR expanded its U.S. presence in 1882 with the acquisition of Great Western Railway, an Ontario road that also had a line from Detroit to Grand Haven, Michigan crossing GTR's existing line at Durand; part of this line, from Detroit to Pontiac, had been in operation since 1838.

With the Great Western routes now part of its network, and with a line to Chicago, GTR was in a position to offer robust competition to the Vanderbilt roads (New York Central & Hudson River, Michigan Central, and Lake Shore & Michigan Southern). Yet GTR still depended on ferries to move freight cars across the St. Clair River between Sarnia,

Ontario, and Port Huron, Michigan, and across the Detroit River between Windsor and Detroit. GTR had two steam-powered car ferries carrying railcars between Sarnia and Port Huron, but as traffic grew another solution had to be found. In 1884 the St. Clair Frontier Tunnel Company was incorporated to build and operate a bore under the river.

After two false starts at tunneling through the blue clay under the river, a relatively new technology—shield tunneling—was applied to the job starting on July 11, 1889. The tunnel, lined with cast iron, opened to revenue traffic on October 24, 1891, and four specially built 0-10-0T tank-type steam engines were used to haul trains between Sarnia and Port Huron. After the deaths of 10 employees from asphyxiation in various incidents between 1892 and 1904, however, GTR decided to electrify the tunnel. Six electric locomotives went into service in 1908, and three more were acquired in later years. They continued to operate until electrification was discontinued in 1958.

CN 1953 system pocket calendar depicting GTW F3 No. 9020. *Author collection*

Until 1900 GTR's lines west of the St. Clair and Detroit Rivers were operated as part of the parent company's system but without a unique identity of their own. On November 22, 1900 the Grand Trunk Western Railway was formed as a holding company for the Michigan properties. Historian Don Hofsommer, author of a history of Grand Trunk Corporation, notes that this was a financial arrangement, not a managerial one. But between the operational improvements achieved with the St. Clair Tunnel and the improved financial controls, Hofsommer writes, "the Michigan lines gradually began to pull their own weight, to repay advances made them by the parent, and by midpoint of the first decade in the new century were even prospering."

The prosperity did not last. By the late 1920s, following the creation of Canadian National, the GTW lines had become financial drains on their parent. In 1928 the Grand Trunk Western Railroad was incorporated, with the idea of making this part of the CN system more financially self-sustaining. It was not the last time that CN would reorganize GTW with the objective of improving its profitability.

Like the Central Vermont, GTW hosted several well-known and well-appointed passenger trains that belied the poor financial performance of its freight service. They included the *International Limited,* which had gone into service between Montreal and Chicago in 1900, the *Inter-City Limited* from Montreal to Chicago via Detroit, and the *Maple*

Like parent CN, Grand Trunk Western used a black paint scheme on yard engines. GTW 8204, at Owosso, Michigan, in 1971, is an Alco S4, delivered in 1956. *Collection of George Carpenter*

Leaf between Montreal and Detroit. Prestigious as they were, they were not making money.

There were no dramatic changes in the CN-GTW relationship until 1971, when Grand Trunk Corporation (GTC) was formed as a holding company for GTW, CV, and Duluth, Winnipeg & Pacific (DW&P). All three properties had been managed from Montreal since the formation of CN, or, in the case of GTW, had been managed from Detroit by people sent from Montreal. Putting the U.S. properties in the hands of U.S. managers was one objective of the reorganization, but it was not an end in itself. The idea was to see if these companies could be made profitable. If not, then perhaps they should not remain part of CN.

Heading up the effort was another representative from Montreal, Robert Bandeen.

Bandeen was an agent of change, not a traditionalist. He set out to remake GTC, and in particular GTW, as a stand-alone company, rather than simply as an appendage of CN. A 1972 brochure issued by GTW proclaimed, "We're changing so much we're becoming a new railroad. New Management is applying new, far-reaching philosophies and methods to Grand Trunk's operations everywhere, in every way. New Services are being instituted, to handle shipments faster and more conveniently for our customers."

There was a certain amount of hyperbole in these claims, but also a lot of truth. GTW had to change: its operating ratio, 119 percent in 1971 and 140 percent the year before, was unacceptable. Furthermore, its customers, most notably General Motors, were insisting it change.

St. Clair Tunnel Company No. 1306, shown here at Sarnia, Ontario, in 1908, was constructed by Baldwin Locomotive Works and Westinghouse in 1907 as one of a group of six locomotives that were placed into service in 1908 and retired in 1959. *John Boyd/National Archives of Canada/PA-060704*

Grand Trunk Western, along with Santa Fe and several other railroads, used Chicago's Dearborn Street Station as a passenger terminal. GTW passenger GP9 No. 4919 is shown here at Dearborn Street in September 1966. *Thomas M. Murray. Author collection*

Bandeen did not stay in Detroit long. In 1972 he returned to Montreal as executive vice president of CN (while remaining responsible for the GTC experiment), and in 1974 he became CEO of Canadian National. He continued as president of GTC until January 1, 1976, when he reorganized CN into profit centers. Succeeding him in the top spot at GTC was John Burdakin, a former Penn Central officer whom Bandeen had initially recruited to be GTW's vice president of operations.

By the late 1970s Grand Trunk Western was generating positive operating income. In 1978 GTW filed a proposal with the Interstate Commerce Commission to acquire

the Detroit, Toledo & Ironton Railroad (DT&I), which ran from Detroit south through Ohio to Cincinnati. GTW acquired DT&I in June 1980. The following year, GTW bought out Norfolk & Western's 50 percent interest in Detroit & Toledo Shore Line (D&TSL) (GTW already owned the other 50 percent). DT&I was initially treated as a separate subsidiary of GTC, but in December 1983 it was folded into GTW.

Surrounded by ever-larger competitors, GTW looked for ways to expand its reach. An opportunity came along in 1981 when the trustee of the bankrupt Milwaukee Road, which had abandoned its Pacific Coast extension,

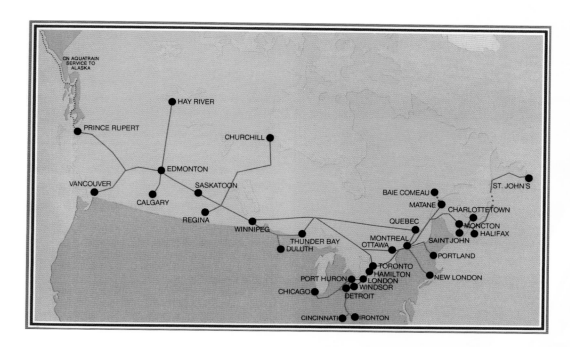

This system map, published soon after the acquisition of Detroit, Toledo & Ironton in 1980, shows the CN network's principal routes at the time. *Author collection*

started to look for a potential buyer of the railroad's remaining assets. One of those assets consisted of trackage rights on the Burlington Northern between St. Paul and Duluth, Minnesota. Acquiring the Milwaukee Road would give GTC and parent CN an all-U.S. route south of the Great Lakes.

While a deal to acquire the Milwaukee Road was in the works, the two carriers negotiated a voluntary coordination agreement that made the Milwaukee the preferred U.S. partner for traffic flowing off the CN system into the U.S. Midwest. In 1983 Chicago & North Western made a competing offer for Milwaukee's assets, and early in 1984

Canadian Pacific's U.S. affiliate, Soo Line, also made an offer. The bidding got too rich for GTC, which dropped out of the contest, and in 1985 Soo Line ended up with the Milwaukee Road. The purchase set in motion a chain of events that would lead, 16 years later, to CN's acquisition of the former Soo Line routes in Wisconsin and Michigan, which by that time were part of Wisconsin Central.

Despite its disappointments in the merger game, GTW was making progress financially, and CN was no longer thinking about selling GTW. As the CN annual report for 1990 put it, Grand Trunk Corporation was "strategically placed to play an important role for Canadian

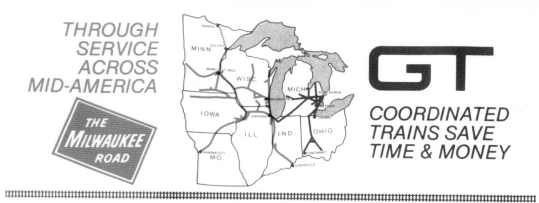

As part of its effort to promote the voluntary coordination agreement with the Milwaukee Road, GTW had scratch pads printed bearing this map. However, Milwaukee Road was not destined to become part of the CN system map. *Author collection*

National in the free trade era." On January 1, 1992 GTC was reintegrated with parent CN as part of "CN North America." GTW, CV, and DW&P retained their identities as operating companies, but there would be a single corporate brand name.

On Dec. 17, 1992 U.S. President George Bush, Canadian Prime Minister Brian Mulroney, and Mexican President Carlos Salinas signed the North American Free Trade Agreement (NAFTA) in separate ceremonies in the three capitals. The trade agreement made it clear to any doubters that CN must have a U.S. presence in order to participate in growing north-south commerce.

CN affirmed its commitment to keeping GTW as part of its network when it decided to invest $155 million in a new St. Clair River Tunnel, one large enough to accommodate high-cube auto-parts cars, multilevel auto racks, and double-stack intermodal equipment. The new tunnel opened in April 1995.

The GTW of today is a slimmed-down version of the railroad it once was. Essentially, it consists of the line from Durand to Chicago, plus the Durand–Detroit–Port Huron triangle and the former D&TSL route to Toledo. DT&I was sold to RailAmerica in 1997, which now operates it as the Indiana & Ohio Railway.

A GTW transfer job with a cut of yellow-door newsprint cars approaches Brighton Park crossing in Chicago in August 1974. GTW 1514 and 1513 were part of a group of eight SW1200 units delivered in 1960. *Tom Murray*

With the acquisition of Illinois Central and Wisconsin Central in 1999 and 2001, respectively, GTW was no longer an appendage of the CN system. It was now a key link in the Canadian National network.

Duluth, Winnipeg & Pacific Railway

Of CN's lines in the United States, the Duluth, Winnipeg & Pacific is the shortest, at 167 miles (269 kilometers), and the youngest. Its predecessor, the Duluth, Rainy Lake & Winnipeg Railway was built in stages from 1901 to 1908, and in the latter it year came under the control of Canadian Northern Railway. CNoR created the Duluth, Winnipeg & Pacific Railway in 1909, and completed the route to Duluth in 1912. At its north end in Ranier, Minnesota, (just east of International Falls), DW&P crosses the Rainy River to connect at Fort Frances, Ontario, with the former CNoR line between Winnipeg and Thunder Bay.

Originally built to carry timber from the white pine forests of northern Minnesota, DW&P carried on in obscurity for many years. It lacked the celebrated passenger trains of GTW or CV, but it gave CN a means of reaching the U.S. Midwest through connections at Duluth with Great Northern and Northern Pacific (later combined into Burlington Northern), Milwaukee Road, Soo Line, and Chicago & North Western.

The DW&P is a pipeline for western Canadian products moving to U.S. Midwestern markets. Here a train composed largely of forest products heads south out of Virginia, Minnesota, in June 1974, with two CN GP9 units in charge. This train, operating as 1st 732, carries green flags to indicate that another section of the same schedule can be expected to follow. *Tom Murray*

If DW&P lacked glamour, it at least made money. When Grand Trunk Corporation was formed in 1971, part of the motivation was that by filing a consolidated tax return, the losses at GTW and CV would insulate DW&P's profits from U.S. income taxes. One reason that DW&P was generating income was that it was ideally situated to serve as a conduit for the resources that Canada was sending to the United States in ever-increasing volumes. Forest products, potash, sulfur, and liquefied petroleum gas (butane and propane) all moved from western Canada via the DW&P to consumers in the United States. Historian Don Hofsommer notes that in the second half of the 1970s, DW&P's average operating ratio was a "most agreeable 65.9."

The importance of DW&P was highlighted in the 1980s and 1990s when CN entered into a series of coordination agreements and haulage contracts with U.S. carriers to move traffic south of Duluth. The first was with Milwaukee Road; then, in 1992, a haulage agreement with Burlington Northern gave CN what amounted to single-line service from western Canada all the way to Chicago. A similar arrangement with Wisconsin Central was negotiated in 1998, and its success led to Wisconsin Central becoming part of CN in 2001.

DW&P was again the center of attention in late 2003 when CN announced that it had reached agreement to buy a package of railroads and a fleet of eight Great Lakes vessels from Great Lakes Transportation (GLT). These properties, at one time operated by U.S. Steel, included the Duluth, Missabe & Iron Range Railway (DM&IR). To reach former Wisconsin Central trackage at South Itasca Yard in Superior, Wisconsin, DW&P had been using trackage rights on DM&IR from Nopeming Junction, a distance of 17 miles (27 kilometers).

The GLT transaction would not only give CN ownership of that segment, but also

would give it two parallel lines—one DW&P and one DM&IR—between Virginia, Minnesota (roughly at the midpoint of the DW&P) and Duluth. This, said CN, would let it run southbound trains over one line and northbound trains over the other, increasing capacity and helping to avoid costly signaling and track improvements on the DW&P.

The GLT transaction would bring other assets (including the Bessemer & Lake Erie Railroad) into the CN family, but the motivation for the deal was to improve the capacity of the DW&P so that it could continue to provide efficient transportation of Canadian resources into the United States.

DWP 3613, an RS11, switches cars in the yard at Virginia, Minnesota, the midpoint of the railroad, in June 1974. *Tom Murray*

CN 5026, on a DW&P train detouring over the Duluth, Missabe & Iron Range Railway, is shown side by side with DM&IR No. 305 at Iron Junction, Minnesota, in August 1992. *Steve Glischinski*

In 2003 CN entered into an agreement with Great Lakes Transportation to acquire several rail and water carriers. The centerpiece of the deal was GLT's Duluth, Missabe & Iron Range Railway, whose operations are to be coordinated with those of its neighbor, CN's Duluth, Winnipeg & Pacific. Here, DM&IR and DW&P trains meet at Steelton, Minnesota, in March 2000. *Steve Glischinski*

CHAPTER SEVEN

PRIVATIZATION AND EXPANSION

In 1981, Robert Bandeen's last full year as CEO, CN earned an operating profit of $193 million. The company was addressing the rapid growth of bulk commodity traffic (coal, sulfur, potash, and grain) in the West by installing double track, extending sidings, and replacing timber bridges on key segments, particularly between Edmonton and Jasper, Alberta, through the Yellowhead Pass, and into British Columbia.

A westbound CN train to Vancouver at Lasha, British Columbia, in April 1996, makes the railway seem tiny in comparison with the works of nature. *Phil Mason*

CN signed an agreement in 1981 to transport coal originating at mines in northern British Columbia. CN would carry the coal from the BC Rail interchange at Prince George to the port of Prince Rupert. At an expected annual volume of more than 9 million tons, it was, as the 1981 annual report noted, "the largest amount of traffic ever to be contracted for by CN Rail."

Where Will CN Get Its Capital?

However, Bandeen's departure from CN coincided with a recession that turned the black ink on CN's ledger to red. As his successor, the government chose 55-year-old Maurice LeClair, a physician who had come to CN in 1979 after serving in a series of high-level government positions. In early 1983 in his first annual report as CEO,

LeClair talked about the historic role of CN, which had been "to weld a number of railway companies into one strong and commercially competitive enterprise serving the entire nation. Though the world in which CN must function has changed dramatically in the intervening years," he stated, "the mission of the company remains tied to its historic role."

By the following year CN had returned to profitability, but the tone of LeClair's message was different. In one year, from 1982 to 1983, the volume of rail traffic in Canada had increased more than 11 percent. CN had been financing its capital investments partly by generating cash internally and partly by borrowing. Yet the borrowing could not continue. Over the next five years the company forecast capital investments of $5 billion, of which almost half would have to come from sources outside the company. "The most pressing problem facing the Corporation in the short term," LeClair wrote, "is the lack of capital needed to finance the improvement and expansion of a number of nationally-important services, most particularly railway

After the Crowsnest grain rate structure was ended, and consolidation of grain elevators had started to make the grain transport system more efficient, CN was motivated to put more maintenance dollars into its grain-gathering network. This welded rail train is west of Saskatoon in July 1994, on the CN Rosetown Subdivision, part of the former Canadian Northern's Saskatoon–Calgary line. *Phil Mason*

services in Western Canada . . . . Means must soon be found to provide new equity capital for the Corporation."

In 1986 two changes occurred: LeClair resigned and the word "privatization" started to appear in discussions about CN's future. In his outgoing message as chairman and CEO, LeClair said, "Canadian National cannot be both an instrument of public policy *at any cost* and a profitable, commercially sound business. . . . A large portion of the company's debt is attributable to public duties for which compensation is non-compensatory or non-existent." Although privatization was now being considered, he said, "CN must be fit and healthy before it can be offered as a candidate for private-sector investment."

In 1992 CN negotiated a haulage agreement with Burlington Northern: BN would handle CN's trains between Chicago and Duluth using CN power and BN crews. This lasted until 1998, when CN moved its Chicago-Duluth traffic to Wisconsin Central. In April 1996 a westbound CN haulage train operates along the Mississippi River near Savanna, Illinois. *Brian Solomon*

Incoming CEO Ronald Lawless, who had served as president of CN Rail after stints in operations and marketing, noted, "Railways are capital intensive. No matter how efficiently they are run, they need an ongoing reinvestment to perpetuate themselves." Yet without equity capital to support this reinvestment, CN had adopted a strategy of downsizing its physical plant and cutting

CN No. 2437, a General Electric Dash 8-40CM, was making one of its first visits to the West in December 1992, and wearing the "CN North America" map paint scheme as it arrived at Jasper, Alberta, with a westbound train. *Phil Mason*

costs wherever possible. CN, Lawless said, was becoming "a smaller, busier, financially stronger railway." The need to get smaller was captured in a single statistic, repeated often by CN management: two-thirds of the railway carried only 10 percent of its business.

The short-line phenomenon that had been going on in the United States for more than a decade did not catch on in Canada until the late 1980s, when CN finally began spinning off some of the lines that carried respectable volumes of traffic but were not generating an adequate return on capital. Lines in Alberta and Ontario were sold to regional rail operators, as was the GT line between Portland, Maine, and the Canadian border. A

CN line between Montreal and Massena, New York, was taken over by Conrail.

CN was also slimming down as a corporation. Marine operations in eastern Canada became a separate crown corporation. The trucking subsidiary, CN Route, was sold. Hotels, including the crown jewels—the Chateau Laurier in Ottawa and the Jasper

The CN North America logo was applied not just to new locomotives, but also to older equipment as well. Here it adorns Central Vermont GP38AC No. 5806. *Brian Solomon*

In the 1990s traffic volumes on CN's Edmonton-Vancouver corridor made it the railway's second-highest volume route. Here, four westbound trains are ready to depart Boston Bar, British Columbia, in April 1995. Today, Boston Bar sees westbound trains of both CN and CP, due to a paired track arrangement between the two railways. Eastbound trains of both railways pass through North Bend on the opposite side of the Fraser River. *Phil Mason*

Park Lodge—were sold to Canadian Pacific, as was CN's interest in CNCP Telecommunications. Proceeds from the sales were used to pay down debt, which put CN's debt-to-capital ratio into a range that was, once again, comparable to that of other large transportation companies. By 1988 CN's principal non-transportation activities consisted of its oil and gas exploration subsidiary, a real estate unit that pursued both development and land sales, the CANAC consultancy, and CN Tower in Toronto.

Meanwhile, growth on CN's core rail network—the one-third that carried 90 percent of the traffic—continued. The Crowsnest rate issue had been resolved a couple of years earlier, and the grain transportation system was benefiting from new, high-capacity covered hopper cars and from investment in track and support systems. About one-third of the route between Edmonton and Vancouver had been

double-tracked. Domestic intermodal traffic between the Maritimes and central Canada increased 41 percent from 1985 to 1986 thanks to CN's acquisition of new tri-axle trailers.

Grand Trunk Corporation had been formed to focus attention on the financial contribution of the company's U.S. subsidiaries, but effective January 1, 1992, GTC was brought back into the CN fold as part of an effort to project a new image: CN North America. The move, said management, reflected the fact that "the domestic freight transportation marketplace has become continental in scope." Locomotives began to appear with a map of North American integrated with the company's famous "noodle" logo. The new image did not last long, but it foreshadowed the expansion of CN's U.S. presence over the next decade.

In 1992 two events reinforced the image of CN as a North American transportation company. CN began construction on a new tunnel between Sarnia, Ontario, and Port Huron, Michigan, to replace the original St. Clair Tunnel opened in 1891. The new tunnel would be able to accommodate not only the modern cars used to serve the auto industry, which for years had been ferried across the river, but also double-stack equipment, which had become the cornerstone of the intermodal business in North America. CN also negotiated a haulage agreement with Burlington Northern (BN) for the movement of CN trains between Duluth and Chicago, making CN trains a common sight on the BN route along the Mississippi River. This agreement enabled CN to offer single-line service between western Canada and Chicago and reduced its dependence on intermediate carriers.

In CN's 1991 annual report, Lawless noted that, "Despite a 47-percent productivity improvement over the past five years, CN remains a relatively high-cost carrier compared with railway competitors, many of whom matched or exceeded CN's productivity growth during the same period."

Tellier Takes Charge

Lawless retired from CN on June 30, 1992. Prime Minister Brian Mulroney caught CN employees and almost every other stakeholder in the company by surprise when he named a long-time civil servant, Paul Tellier, to succeed Lawless. Most recently Tellier had served as clerk of the Privy Council and secretary of the Cabinet, making him in effect Canada's top government bureaucrat.

Tellier took over on October 1, 1992, and almost from the beginning it was clear that he had a different management style than CN employees were accustomed to. "Urgency" and "impatience" were two of the more polite words used to describe his approach to CN's challenges. "Change must occur more quickly," Tellier stated. "Entrenched habits and attitudes must be replaced by more productive methods

CN SD40 5134 is the leading unit on eastbound train No. 408 crossing the Canso Strait at Port Hastings, Nova Scotia, at the south end of Cape Breton Island, in September 1993. The following month, the Cape Breton & Central Nova Scotia Railway began operating the line between Truro and Sydney. *Phil Mason*

CN 5314 and a Bombardier HR616 lead an eastbound train over the Continental Divide at Yellowhead, British Columbia, in July 1995. (Bombardier took over Montreal Locomotive Works in 1979 and subsequently exited the locomotive business.) The elevation at Yellowhead is only 3,720 feet (1,128 meters), compared with 5,332 feet (1,618 meters) at Canadian Pacific's crossing of Kicking Horse Pass. *Phil Mason*

and a clearer-sighted perspective. In short, CN will have to break with the past—or risk losing the future."

Tellier set out to reduce CN's payroll by 11,000 people over a three-year period. It took him a little longer than that, but by 1996 the company's workforce stood at just over 24,000, versus 35,300 in 1992. The trackage operated by CN was whittled down, too, through abandonments as well as sales and leases to regional operators. In 1992 the company had operated 19,522 route miles

(31,430 kilometers); by the end of 1995 it was reduced to 17,918 miles (28,848 kilometers). CN also set up "internal short lines" in areas where labor unions would agree to modified work rules.

The new CEO also restructured senior management, bringing in new people, obtaining resignations from some long-time employees, and flattening the organizational chart. In the words of one senior executive, "While Bandeen had made major strides in changing the financial structure to enable a profit-motivated, business-like approach, many in senior management still had a crown corporation mentality. Tellier added the final piece to the puzzle by replacing the entire executive team with people who would march to his drum and drive home the bottom-line approach. The strategy was to fix the costs, then the service, and finally grow the revenue."

Privatization

Even though CN was becoming a smaller railway, it was carrying more traffic, and doing so more profitably. From 1992 to 1995 revenue ton-miles increased 9 percent and operating income (excluding special charges) rose from $112 million to $552 million. The stage was set for the privatization of Canadian National, and in February 1995 the government announced that it would do exactly that. An initial public offering of CN shares was scheduled, and on November 17, 1995 the company's stock was offered to investors on the Toronto, Montreal, and New York stock exchanges.

The privatization of CN was a momentous event in the history of Canadian enterprise. It was the largest initial public offering of stock in the history of the country. But the most shocking thing to Canadians was that CN, which many still thought of as an arm of the government, was being turned into an investor-owned company. Harry Bruce, in his book about the CN privatization, *The Pig That Flew,* writes that Americans "had a stronger faith in CN's future than the

In October 1999 CN train No. 305 has just crossed from New Brunswick into Quebec at Courchesne, on the former National Transcontinental route that now serves as CN's mainline between Montreal and the Maritimes. The 148-car train is slogging through the Notre Dame Mountains and cresting the first of three grades between here and Pelletier, 40 miles (64 kilometers) to the west. *George Pitarys*

CN's acquisition of Illinois Central in 1999 and Wisconsin Central in 2001 meant that locomotives of all three railroads could be found in unfamiliar places. Here, IC SD40-3 No. 6203, a former Burlington Northern unit, leads two Wisconsin Central units at New Brighton, Minnesota, in July 2003. *Steve Glischinski*

Canadians, and were therefore willing to pay a higher price for the shares." When the dust settled after the IPO, U.S. investors owned most of the company's stock.

In the first two years of privatization, CN continued to make gains in efficiency and financial strength. Tellier had set an objective of 85 percent for the operating ratio, which in 1992 stood at 97.5 percent. By 1996 that ratio had, in fact, been reduced to 85 percent, and then to 82 percent in 1996 and 79 percent in 1997. Operating income for 1997 was $927 million. Route mileage shrank to 15,292 miles (24,620 kilometers) in 1997, but revenue ton-miles increased by another 13 percent from 1995 to 1997.

Privatization finally freed CN management from the need to look over its shoulder to see what politicians and bureaucrats thought about its business activities. Though it still operated under government regulations in both Canada and the United States, privatization put CN on the same basis vis-à-vis government as its competitors and connecting lines in the rail industry.

CN to the Gulf: Illinois Central

Tellier knew that the future of North American transportation lay in north-south trade. NAFTA had eased trade restrictions among Canada, the United States, and Mexico. Tellier wanted to ensure that CN got its share of the resulting rail traffic. In February 1998 CN confirmed widespread speculation that it was negotiating to buy Illinois Central Railroad (IC), which would extend CN's reach to the Gulf of Mexico. Three months later CN and Kansas City Southern announced a 15-year marketing alliance that would effectively give CN access to Mexico.

One of IC's key assets was its CEO, Hunter Harrison, who had implemented an operating plan based on running trains to schedule. IC offered its customers reliable, consistent service, and it also had the lowest operating ratio of any major railroad. CN had already been working toward the objective of running a "scheduled railroad," particularly with the implementation in 1995 of a new

Resplendent in fall plumage, the orange maples east of Tarte, Quebec, nicely match the colors of SD75 CN 5695, leading train No. 148 in October 2001. Midway between Edmundston and St. André Junction, the siding at Tarte was recently lengthened as part of CN's $24 million capital project to improve times on its Halifax-Montreal service. *George Pitarys*

GTW SD40-3 No. 5943 and WC SD45 No. 7506 are on the head end of CN train No. 406 at Shoreview, Minnesota, in December 2003. The WC unit was formerly owned by BN. The GTW unit has a more interesting past. Originally CN SD40 No. 5102, it was rebuilt by Alstom Transport for Kansas City Southern. CN then leased it and renumbered it for GTW. *Steve Glischinski*

computer system called SRS (Service Reliability Strategy). SRS was based on technology acquired from the Santa Fe Railway, but CN had tailored it to meet its own needs and operating conditions.

Tellier wasted no time bringing Harrison on board. In March 1998, more than a year before CN was able to complete its acquisition of IC, Harrison joined CN as its chief operating officer. He, in turn, wasted no time developing a new operating plan for Canadian National aimed at increasing the reliability of CN's service; improving the utilization of cars, locomotives, and train crews; and reducing operating costs. The new plan was put into practice on September 6, 1998.

In July 1999 CN completed its acquisition of IC, but Tellier had bigger ambitions. In December of that year, he announced that CN would merge with Burlington Northern Santa Fe (BNSF). Despite talk about a "merger of equals," and the fact that BNSF's revenues were more than twice CN's, CN was clearly in the driver's seat on the proposed merger. The surviving company, to be called North American Railways, Inc., would be based in Montreal and its top two officers would be Paul Tellier and Hunter Harrison.

The CN-BNSF combination was not to be, however. Four railroads—Canadian Pacific, CSX, Norfolk Southern, and Union Pacific—mounted a vigorous campaign to stop the deal. The Surface Transportation Board (the U.S. regulator of rail mergers) called a time out to examine the larger issue of industry consolidation. In July 2000 CN and BNSF called off the merger.

Opposite: CN train No. 406 passes through Arden Hills, Minnesota, with a CN SD60F and two WC SD45 units, in November 2003. *Steve Glischinski*

Completing the Iron Lariat: Wisconsin Central

One of the missing links in the CN network, a gap made all the more noticeable with IC added to the CN route map, was between Duluth (the south end of the Duluth, Winnipeg & Pacific) and Chicago. CN's first attempt to create what some called an "iron lariat" around the Great Lakes had been in the early 1980s when Grand Trunk made overtures to buy the assets of the bankrupt Milwaukee Road. That bid fell short and the Milwaukee Road ended up in the hands of Canadian Pacific's U.S. affiliate, Soo Line.

The Soo-Milwaukee transaction rendered much of the Soo Line's trackage in the upper Midwest surplus. Those routes became

Maritimes-bound train No. 306 rolls through Ste. Perpetue, Quebec, on the St. Lawrence River plain, in May 2003. Dairy farming is a large part of this area's local economy, and one in which the railway still has a role, serving a nearby feed dealer. *George Pitarys*

the core of a new regional railroad, Wisconsin Central (WC), which began its life in October 1987. WC soon established a reputation for efficiency and customer service. In 1998 CN negotiated a haulage agreement with WC under which WC crews would handle CN trains between Duluth and Chicago, replacing a similar agreement with BNSF.

In January 2001 CN announced that it would buy Wisconsin Central; the transaction was completed in October of that year. However, the WC deal came with some international baggage. WC's president, Edward Burkhardt, had worked to apply the WC management philosophy and business model in countries whose railways were

emerging from government ownership. As a result WC had developed a portfolio of overseas rail investments. Its New Zealand and Australia interests were disposed of within six months of the CN-WC merger. However, a poorly executed privatization plan on the British rail network had reduced the marketability of the WC property there, known as the English, Welsh & Scottish Railway. CN kept the EW&S shares on its books, although it remained hopeful that it could find a buyer for them.

The WC transaction also brought one Canadian property into the CN family: the former Algoma Central Railway from Sault Ste. Marie to Hearst, Ontario, which WC had acquired in 1995.

Scheduled Railroading Makes CN an Industry Leader

The benefits of the new operating plan implemented in late 1998 were evident to anyone who watched CN's operations or read its financial statements. With Illinois Central included, CN had an operating ratio of 75 percent in 1998. The next year, it was down to 72 percent; the following year, just under 70 percent. The company had become the most efficient major railway in North America. By early 2001 Harrison reported that CN had reduced the size of its locomotive fleet from almost 2,000 units to 1,260. The company began to negotiate new labor agreements with its train and engine service employees in the United States, based on hourly compensation instead of the time-honored mileage basis of pay. Harrison said the change could allow CN to reduce its employment in the running trades by as much as one-third.

Thanks to the scheduled railroad, customers were rewarding CN with more of their freight. From 1998 to 2000, the last full year before the merger with WC, revenue ton-miles increased almost 8 percent. By 2002, with WC now part of the CN system, RTMs were up another 7 percent over the 2000 figure.

CN had become an industry leader in efficiency and customer service. Thanks to the effect of these operational improvements on the company's net income and cash flow, CN was also rewarded with gains in its share price that far outpaced most other stocks. From the time it went public in November 1995 through December 31, 2003, the stock generated a return of 507 percent.

Into the Twenty-first Century

The Tellier era at CN came to a close at the end of 2002, 10 years after it began. CN's CEO left to take a similar position with Bombardier, a Canadian manufacturer of railcars, aircraft, and recreational equipment. Chief operating officer Hunter Harrison moved into the top slot, effective January 1, 2003. Although they were different in personality and background, Tellier and Harrison had worked well together over the preceding five years. What they had in common was a sense of urgency and an inability to be satisfied with the status quo.

Soon after Harrison moved up to CEO, CN launched another program aimed at reducing costs while making service more consistent. The "Intermodal Excellence"

The Ultramar refinery at St. Romauld, Quebec, ships a daily tank train of gasoline to Montreal. In May 2003 CN train No. 782 with the Ultramar empties crosses the Nicolet River in St. Leonard D'Aston, Quebec, en route back to the refinery. *George Pitarys*

In the fall of 2003, CN announced that it had been selected by British Columbia to operate the provincially owned BC Rail. CN will lease the railway and integrate it with its existing British Columbia operations. *BC Rail*

On Dec 31, 2003, CN train No. 406 rolls across the 185-foot-high St. Croix River Bridge near Somerset, Wisconsin. The bridge was placed into service in 1911 by Soo Line, the U.S. affiliate of Canadian Pacific. In the 1980s this line (between Minneapolis and Stevens Point, Wisconsin) became part of Wisconsin Central, which was acquired by CN in 2001. Writer and photographer David Plowden has called this "one of the world's most beautiful steel structures." *Steve Glischinski*

initiative was intended to smooth out the peaks and valleys of container and trailer shipments, and to keep intermodal traffic moving rather than allowing it to fill up yards and terminals. The initiative involved running fewer, more consistently sized trains, requiring reservations for slots on each train, pricing according to customer demand on various days of the week, and reducing the use of CN facilities for container and trailer storage. Initially implemented in the Halifax–Montreal–Toronto–Windsor corridor, it was subsequently expanded across Canada.

CN continued its search for expansion possibilities under Harrison, although one acquisition that was being negotiated when he took over had to be scuttled. The Province of Ontario was interested in selling the Ontario Northland Railway, and CN was the logical buyer. With an election imminent, the province insisted on labor guarantees that CN could not agree to, and in June 2003 the company said it was walking away from the Ontario Northland transaction.

CN's next deal, announced in October 2003 and completed in May 2004, was the acquisition of several former U.S. Steel rail and water carriers from Great Lakes Transportation. These included a fleet of eight Great Lakes ore vessels, a dock operation in Ohio, and the Bessemer & Lake Erie Railroad. CN's real reason for acquiring this package was that it included the Duluth, Missabe & Iron Range Railway. CN's DW&P unit already used trackage rights over DM&IR as a critical link in its access to Duluth. By combining these two carriers, CN could implement a paired-track arrangement north of Duluth to increase capacity and hold down capital investment.

In November 2003 CN issued another major announcement, this time at Victoria, British Columbia, where the provincial government had selected CN to lease and operate the government-owned BC Rail. CN had competed with Canadian Pacific (and with a partnership between BNSF and regional rail operator OmniTRAX) for the BC Rail franchise. It was a controversial award; labor was fearful of job losses, and some in British Columbia felt that the railway was part of the province's patrimony, not to be given away to an outsider like CN (most of whose owners were U.S. investors). CN tried to mollify the opponents by agreeing to make significant investments in all of its British Columbia rail operations, including a clearance improvement program on the Prince Rupert line.

EPILOGUE

Canadian National has come a long way since its inception as a government-run collection of financially troubled railways.

Many of the changes at CN have reflected rail industry trends. Every North American railway has experienced dieselization, the increased use of computers, centralization of dispatching and numerous other functions, as well as dramatic improvements in productivity.

But CN started out in a different place—and has reached a different place—than any of its peers. It started as a collection of capital-starved railways and for several decades its owners, the people of Canada, looked to it to provide social services more than they wanted it to provide efficient transportation.

Through the efforts of one generation of leaders and employees after another, CN was transformed into a modern business enterprise and, most recently, into a standard-setter for the rail industry.

CN was fortunate to have people like Sir Henry Thornton, Donald Gordon, Robert Bandeen, Ronald Lawless, and Paul Tellier lead it during transitional periods, when a clear vision of the future was required. Each of these men left CN a stronger, more capable company than he had found it, even when that strength was not reflected in the cold numbers on the financial statements.

CN has done more than survive. It has prevailed.

SOURCES

Books

Bruce, Harry. *The Pig That Flew: The Battle to Privatize Canadian National*. Vancouver: Douglas & McIntyre, 1997.

Burrows, Roger G. *Railway Mileposts: British Columbia, Vol. I: The CPR Mainline Route From the Rockies to the Pacific Including the Okanagan Route and CN's Canyon Route*. North Vancouver, B.C.: Railway Milepost Books, 1981.

Clegg, Anthony and Ray Corley. *Canadian National Steam Power*. Montreal: Trains & Trolleys, 1969.

Currie, A. W. *The Grand Trunk Railway in Canada*. Toronto: University of Toronto Press, 1957.

Dubin, Arthur D. *More Classic Trains*. Milwaukee, Wis.: Kalmbach Publishing Co., 1974.

Fournier, Leslie T. *Railway Nationalization in Canada: The Problem of the Canadian National Railways*. Toronto: The Macmillan Company, 1935.

Gilbert, Clare. *St. Clair Tunnel: Rails Beneath the River*. Toronto: Stoddart Publishing Co., 1991.

Hastings, Philip R. *Grand Trunk Heritage: Steam in New England*. New York: Railroad Heritage Press, 1978.

Hofsommer, Don L. *Grand Trunk Corporation: Canadian National Railways in the United States, 1971–1992*. East Lansing, Mich.: Michigan State University Press, 1995.

Love, J. A. *Canadian National in the West, Vols. One, Two and Three*. Calgary, Alta.: B.R.M.N.A., 1980, 1981, 1983.

Lowe, J. Norman. *Canadian National in the East, Vols. One, Two and Three*. Calgary, Alta.: B.R.M.N.A., 1981, 1983, 1985.

MacKay, Donald. *The People's Railway: A History of the Canadian National*. Vancouver: Douglas & McIntyre, 1992.

MacKay, Donald and Lorne Perry. *Train Country: An Illustrated History of Canadian National Railways*. Vancouver: Douglas & McIntyre, 1994.

McDonnell, Greg. *The History of Canadian Railroads*. London: New Burlington Books, 1985.

Middleton, William D. *Landmarks on the Iron Road: Two Centuries of North American Railroad Engineering*. Bloomington, Ind.: Indiana University Press, 1999.

——. *When the Steam Railroads Electrified*. Milwaukee, Wis.: Kalmbach Publishing Co., 1974.

Plowden, David. *Bridges: The Spans of North America*. New York: W. W. Norton & Company, 2002.

Stevens, G. R. *Canadian National Railways, Vol. I: Sixty Years of Trial and Error (1839–1896)*. Toronto: Clarke, Irwin & Company, 1960.

——. *Canadian National Railways, Vol. II: Towards the Inevitable (1896–1922)*. Toronto: Clarke, Irwin & Company, 1962.

——. *History of the Canadian National Railways*. New York: The Macmillan Company, 1973.

Turner, Robert D. *Vancouver Island Railroads*. San Marino, Calif.: Golden West Books, 1973.

Other Publications

Barriger, John Walker. *Sir Henry Thornton, K.B.E. (1871–1933) Pioneer*. New York: The Newcomen Society of England, American Branch, 1948.

Canada on the Move: The Canadian Railroads Modernize for an Expanding Nation. *Modern Railroads*, July 1952.

Canadian National Railways locomotive roster. *Extra 2200 South: The Locomotive Newsmagazine*, issues 48–50, 1974–1975.

CN Lines Special Interest Group, *CN Lines Magazine*, various issues.

Lavallée, Omer. The Grand Trunk Railway of Canada: An Overview. *Railroad History*, Issue 147, Autumn 1982.

The Official Guide of the Railways, various issues. New York: National Railway Publication Company.

Canadian National and Affiliated Company Materials

Annual reports, 1923–2002
Growing Up With Canada, 1987
Growing With Prince Rupert, undated (ca. 1983)
GT Facts: Basic Information About the Grand Trunk Western Railroad, December 1972
Investor fact books, 1997–2003
Maps and travel brochures
Public and employee timetables
Railway Capacity: CN Rail Transcontinental Route, November 17, 1980

Other Resources

Canada Science and Technology Museum web site, www.sciencetech.technomuses.ca
Canadian National web site, www.cn.ca
Canadian Railway Hall of Fame web site, www.railfame.ca
CN Lines Special Interest Group web site, www.cnlines.com
Eisfeller, Richard. *CN's Northern Ontario Mains*. Video. Greenland, N.H.: Big "E" Productions, 2002.

——. *Paired Track in the Canyons, Parts I and II*. Video. Greenland, N.H.: Big "E" Productions, 2002.

INDEX